2429

FOREWORD

This Golden Guide singles out the phenomena of light and color and describes the scientific concepts in easily understood terms. Light and color are intimately involved in our lives yet a real understanding of their nature is rare. This book presents in simple terms the complex physical, physiological, and psychological aspects of light and color. To condense this subject into this small book required some sacrifice, so many details and qualifying remarks have been omitted, and much of the data has been presented in simplified form.

We are grateful to the individuals and organizations who generously supplied data and loaned pictures for our illustrations and to the authors of the many excellent books which were drawn upon for ideas and information (Bibliography on page 156). We are grateful also to James Hathway, James Skelly, and George Fichter for their editorial assistance and to Dr. Frederick L. Brown for his critical review.

Photo credits: Mt. Wilson & Palomar Observatories, Copyright by California Institute of Technology and Carnegie Institute of Washington, 7, 74, 75; Clarence Rainwater, 30, 56, 79, 92, 93, 95, 97, 119, 144; Enid Kotchnig, 31, 146; Ealing Corp., 46; O. C. Rudolph & Sons, Inc., 54; Yerkes Observatory, 72; Institute for International Research, 96; Florida Development Commission, 99; Roger Behrens, 109; "The Printing Industry" by Victor Strauss, 112; American Optical Co., 116; redrawn from *Scientific American*, 118; from "An Introduction to Color" by R. M. Evans, 120; Munsell Color Co., 127; Container Corp. of America, 129; painting by Louis M. Condax from "The Science of Color," Optical Society of America, 132; The United Piece Dye Works, 140; Western Electric, 142 (bot. left); Edward Diehl, 143; Original Dufaycolor by Blanche Glasgow, American Museum of Photography, 145; Elizabeth Wilcox (Polaroid), 147; National Gallery of Art, Washington, D.C., Chester Dale Collection: detail from Self Portrait, 1889, by Paul Gauguin, 149; Perkin-Elmer Corp., 152 (top); Optics Technology, 152 (bot.).

CONTENTS

Natural light dispersion—a double rainbow

NATURE OF LIGHT AND COLOR

We know the world through our senses: sight, hearing, touch, taste, and smell. Each sense responds to particular stimuli, and the sensations we experience give us information about our surroundings. Sight is the most important of the senses. Through sight we perceive the shape, size, and color of objects; also their distance, motions, and relationships to each other. Light is the stimulus for the sense of sight—the raw material of vision.

To understand the fascinating story of light, let us explore its nature, its manifestation of color, its behavior in lenses and prisms, and then its uses in science and art. This will help in understanding how the sensation of seeing affects our action, our attitudes, our moods, and our daily experiences.

COLOR is the essence of light; light the essence of life. The green pigment of plants plays an essential role in sustaining all life. The colors of many animals blend with their surroundings, hiding the animals from their enemies. Some, like this anole, can even change their colors as they move from one background to another.

4

Man has put light and color to work in many ways. Physicians detect diseases by changes in the color of eyeballs, throat, or skin. The acidity of a solution, the composition of an alloy, the temperature of a furnace, and the velocity of a distant star can be determined by a color or a color change. Decorators choose restful colors for bedrooms, brighter colors for work areas. In advertising, a color entices the consumer to change his brand of breakfast food. Light and color give meaning to everyday contacts between man and his world in many ways.

Light and color involve physical, physiological, and psychological factors. Physicists deal with the energies and frequencies of light waves and the interaction of light with matter. Physiologists study visual processes and psychologists study the effects of visual and color perception. These three groups of scientists developed different viewpoints and different vocabularies in talking about light and color. After long study, a committee of the Optical Society of America reconciled the differences and set up a clearly defined and consistent terminology.

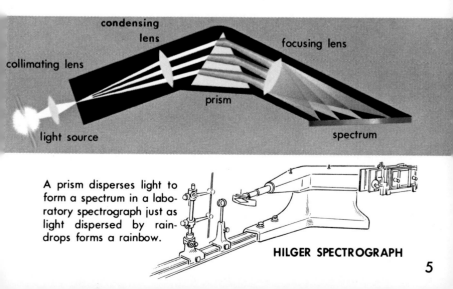

collimating lens

condensing lens

focusing lens

prism

light source

spectrum

A prism disperses light to form a spectrum in a laboratory spectrograph just as light dispersed by raindrops forms a rainbow.

HILGER SPECTROGRAPH

SCIENTIFIC MEASUREMENTS involve large and small numbers, interrelated units, and great precision. Our everyday units of measurement come from the English system with its inches, gallons, and pounds and are convenient to use only because they are familiar. The metric system is favored by scientists because the relationship between units of length, volume, and weight is simpler. The system's use of decimals also makes for faster and more accurate computations. Large numbers can be expressed concisely.

Metric units of length are used in this book. The table below lists some common units, uses, symbols, comparative values in meters and in inches, and common objects of each unit's approximate size.

UNITS OF LENGTH

Unit	Symbol	Equivalent in meters, inches	About the size of
METER measures radio waves	m	1 m 39.37 inches	A small boy
CENTIMETER measures microwaves	cm	.01 m (10^{-2} m) 0.3937 in.	A sunflower seed
MILLIMETER measures microwaves	mm	.001 m (10^{-3} m) .03937 in.	A grain of sand
MICRON measures infrared	μ	.000001 m (10^{-6} m) .000039 in.	A small bacterium
MILLIMICRON measures light waves	mμ	.000000001 m (10^{-9} m) .000000039 in.	A benzene molecule
ANGSTROM measures ultraviolet and light waves	A	.0000000001 m (10^{-10} m) .0000000039 in.	A hydrogen atom

Numbers in this book are often given as powers of 10. For example, 10^3 is 1,000 (read 10^3 as "10 to the third power"; the 3 is called an exponent), and 10^6 is 1,000,000. Negative exponents are fractions or decimals; 10^{-3} is 1/1,000 or .001.

The Andromeda nebula is so far away that light from it takes about two and a half million years to reach the earth. Studies of light from such celestial bodies give clues to the structure of the universe.

THE SPEED OF LIGHT in free space (a vacuum) is 186,282 miles* per second. This seems to be the natural speed limit in the universe. There is good reason to believe that nothing can ever travel faster.

The speed of light in a vacuum is a constant, always denoted by c in equations, as in Einstein's energy equation, $E = mc^2$. No matter what the source of light, or how fast the source and observer are moving with respect to one another, the speed of light in free space is always the same. This remarkable fact is believed to be true only of light. The speed of a bullet, for example, depends in part on the speed of the gun from which it is fired and on the speed of the observer as well. The speed of sound varies with the speed of the measurer but not with the speed of the source. The speed of light is independent of both source and measurer. It is a universal constant, one of the most important constants in all of science. The constancy of the speed of light is a basic postulate of Einstein's theory of relativity.

* Approximately 3×10^8 meters per second

ELECTROMAGNETIC WAVES carry energy in all directions through the universe. All objects receive, absorb, and radiate these waves, which can be pictured as electric and magnetic fields vibrating at right angles to each other and also to the direction in which the wave is traveling. Light is one form of electromagnetic wave. All electromagnetic waves travel in space at the same speed—the speed of light.

Electromagnetic waves show a continuous range of frequencies and wavelengths (pp. 10–11). Frequency is the number of wave crests passing a point in one second. Electromagnetic wave frequencies run from about one per second to over a trillion-trillion (10^{24}) per second. For light, the frequencies are four to eight hundred trillion ($4-8 \times 10^{14}$) waves per second. The frequency times the wavelength gives the speed of the wave. The higher the frequency the shorter the wavelength.

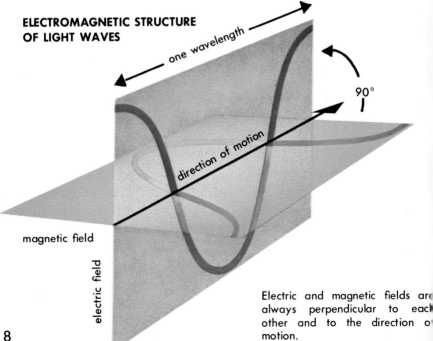

ELECTROMAGNETIC STRUCTURE OF LIGHT WAVES

one wavelength

90°

direction of motion

magnetic field

electric field

Electric and magnetic fields are always perpendicular to each other and to the direction of motion.

A "SNAPSHOT" OF A GREEN LIGHT WAVE

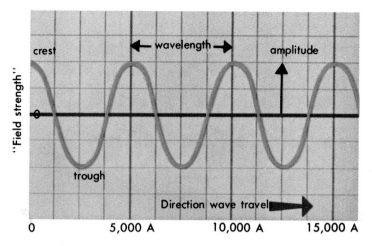

WAVELENGTH is the distance from the crest of one wave to the crest of the next. The height of a wave crest is its amplitude and is related to the energy of the wave. The wave shown in the diagram is a green light wave. Distances are in Angstroms (p. 6).

GAMMA RAYS AND X-RAYS, with wavelengths less than 10A, are penetrating radiations that are absorbed very little in passing through solid matter. The amount of the absorption depends upon the density of the material, so these rays are useful for making shadowgrams (X-ray pictures) of the denser parts of an object.

ULTRAVIOLET RAYS are produced in great quantity by the sun and by special types of lamps. Though not detected by the eye, they do affect photographic film. They also cause suntan. Ordinary glass does not transmit much ultraviolet so you do not tan behind an ordinary window. The wavelengths of ultraviolet rays (10 A to 3,500 A) are longer than those of X-rays but shorter than those of light. A bit longer than light are the waves of infrared radiation which we sense as heat.

frequency in
cycles per second

10^2	10^4	10^6	10^8	10^{10}	10^{12}

power	induction heating	radio waves	infrared rays

3×10^{17}	10^{15}	10^{13}	10^{11}	10^9	10^7	10

wavelength in
Angstrom units

7500 A

VISIBLE

infrared	red	orange	yellow

VISIBLE LIGHT is that portion of the electromagnetic spectrum that normally stimulates the sense of sight. Electromagnetic waves exhibit a continuous range of frequencies and wavelengths. In the visible part of the spectrum these frequencies and wavelengths are what we see as colors. The wavelengths of light range from 3,500 A to 7,500 A. The wavelengths of infrared rays (7,500 A – 10,000,000 A), longer than light rays, are not detected by the eye, and do not appreciably affect ordinary photographic film. They are also called heat or thermal rays and give us the sensation of warmth.

Because all electromagnetic waves are basically alike, we can expect them to behave in a similar manner. Differences are really but a matter of degree and are due to the differences in frequency. Light waves are unique only in their visual effects. The concept of color, for instance, has meaning only in reference to light waves.

ELECTROMAGNETIC SPECTRUM

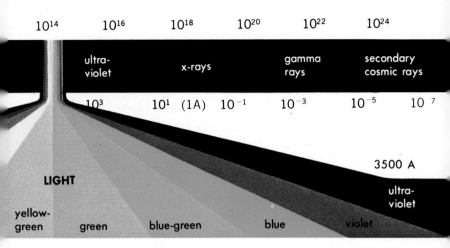

THE ELECTROMAGNETIC SPEC-TRUM, shown above, covers all known radiation of which light is a small but important part.

The expanded visible portion of the electromagnetic spectrum is seen as a continuous gradation in hue from red through violet.

WAVELENGTH OF VISIBLE RAYS

The wavelengths (λ) of visible light are what we see as colors. Red has the longest waves, violet the shortest.

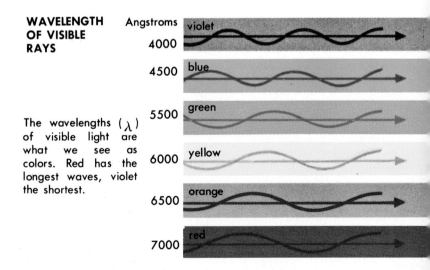

4000 A   4500 A   5000 A   5500 A

Spectrum of sunlight showing

A SPECTROGRAPH (p. 5) separates a beam of light into its component wavelengths and displays them in a spectrum. The spectrum of an incandescent lamp is a continuous band of colors ranging from violet through blue, green, yellow, orange, to red. Each color blends into its neighbors in an unbroken band of wavelengths. Solids, liquids, and gases at very high pressure give continuous spectra if they are made hot enough.

Gases at low pressure have discrete spectra consisting of colored lines or bands with dark spaces between. A gas gives a line spectrum if its molecule consists of a single atom, a band spectrum if it consists of more than one atom. The gas can be identified by the pattern of its spectral lines or bands, and its temperature can be determined by their relative intensities.

TYPES OF SPECTRA

Continuous spectrum of incandescent lamp

Line spectrum of barium

Band spectrum of carbon arc in air

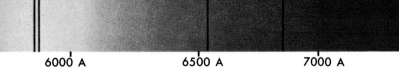

6000 A   6500 A   7000 A

principal Fraunhofer lines (p. 21).

If a line or narrow band of the spectrum is isolated by a slit or by colored filters, the light that comes through is called monochromatic light. It consists of a single wavelength or a very narrow range of wavelengths and excites in the observer a sensation of color, such as red, green, or blue. White light, such as sunlight, is a mixture of all visible wavelengths. An object that reflects all wavelengths equally appears white to our eyes.

Each light source emits a characteristic spectrum which can be plotted on a graph showing how the relative energy varies with the wavelength. This relationship is called the spectral energy distribution curve for the light source. Most sources also give off invisible ultraviolet and infrared radiation, so the complete spectrum usually includes more than just visible light.

SPECTRAL ENERGY DISTRIBUTION CURVES

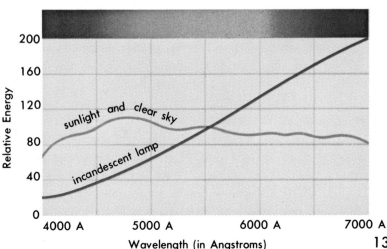

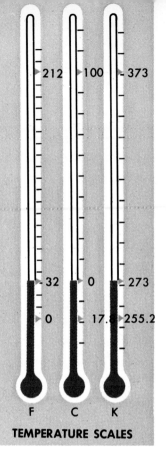

212 ▶100 ▶ 373

32   0   273

0   17.8 ▶255.2

F   C   K
TEMPERATURE SCALES

TEMPERATURE is a measure of the rate of random motions of molecules. Absolute zero is the temperature at which all such motions are at a theoretical minimum. The Kelvin, or absolute, temperature scale, widely used in scientific work, starts at absolute zero. The freezing point of water is 273°K, and the boiling point is 373°K. Equivalent temperatures on the Fahrenheit (F) and Celsius (C) temperature scales are shown at left.

Temperature and the color of a hot object are often closely related. As a piece of iron is heated it changes in color from gray to red, to orange, to yellow, and finally to white.

RADIATION is being continually exchanged between every object and its surroundings. The amount and quality of this radiation depends upon the temperature and material of both the emitter and the absorber. When two objects are at about the same temperature, little heat is transferred between them. When one object is much hotter than the other, heat flows to the colder one. This occurs when you hold out your hand and feel the warmth of a hot stove. Your hand radiates less energy than it receives. The rate at which an object emits this radiant energy is proportional to the fourth power of its Kelvin temperature. Doubling this temperature increases the rate of radiation 16 times.

THE BEST RADIATOR is an absolutely black body. It absorbs all the radiation that falls on it. Every light source is a radiator, but some are more efficient than others. An object that is a good absorber of radiation is also a good emitter.

A small deep hole or cavity in a graphite block serves as a practical black body. Any light that enters the hole is reflected many times from the walls and is partly absorbed at each reflection until no light remains. Thus the hole appears perfectly black. If the walls of the cavity are heated, however, they give off radiation in all directions. The radiation that escapes from the hole is called black-body radiation.

The spectral distribution of radiant energy emitted by a heated black body depends only on its Kelvin temperature, and not at all on the material of which it is made. At low temperature (below 800°K) only infrared radiation results. At about 6,000°K (the temperature of the sun's surface), the peak of the spectral energy curve is near the midpoint of the visible spectrum. Both ultraviolet and infrared radiation also occur.

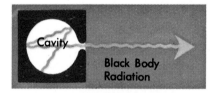

Cavity

Black Body Radiation

The standard unit of light-source intensity, the candle, is 1/60 of the intensity of 1 cm^2 of a black body at the temperature of melting platinum.

ENERGY DISTRIBUTION OF A BLACK BODY

At a given temperature, there is a specific curve that represents the energy distribution of a black body. At higher temperatures, the peak of the curve occurs at shorter wavelengths.

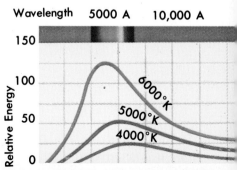

Wavelength 5000 A   10,000 A

Relative Energy

150

100

50

0

6000°K
5000°K
4000°K

COLOR TEMPERATURE may be assigned to any light source by matching it visually against a black-body radiator. The temperature at which the black body matches the color of a light source is said to be the color temperature of the source. For incandescent sources, such as an ordinary household light bulb, the color temperature is related simply to the true temperature and is often approximately equal to it. An observer sees the star Antares, with a color temperature almost 5,000°K, as red. Sirius, at about 11,000°K, is much hotter and appears white. The color temperature of some light sources, however, has nothing whatever to do with the actual temperature. A "daylight" fluorescent tube, for example, may have a rated color temperature of 6,500°K and yet be so cool that it is not uncomfortable to touch.

COLOR-TEMPERATURE CLASSIFICATION OF STARS

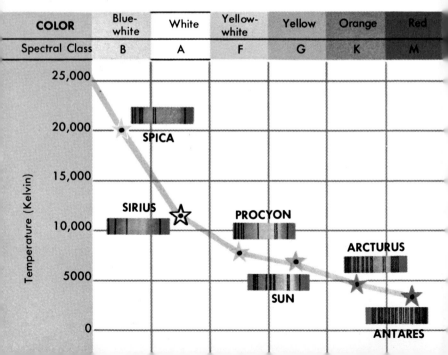

COLOR	Blue-white	White	Yellow-white	Yellow	Orange	Red
Spectral Class	B	A	F	G	K	M

THREE STANDARDIZED LIGHT SOURCES, known as A, B, and C, are used to match colors. Source A approximates ordinary incandescent lamp light, source B noon sunlight, and source C average daylight. The standard incandescent lamp operates at a color temperature of 2,854°K. The other two standard sources are derived from this same lamp by the use of carefully specified filters. Each source may be considered white in particular instances. White light is known to be a mixture of all colors (p. 13). These sources of white light differ because they are made up of different amounts of the various colors.

THE RELATIVE ENERGIES of the three internationally accepted light sources are plotted for the visible region of the spectrum. The curve for the standard incandescent lamp, because of its tungsten filament, is the same as that for a black body at 2,854°K.

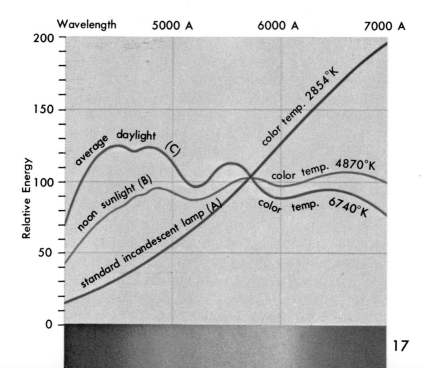

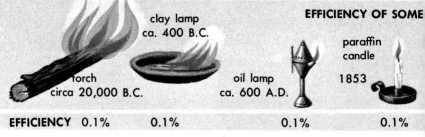

torch
circa 20,000 B.C.

clay lamp
ca. 400 B.C.

oil lamp
ca. 600 A.D.

paraffin
candle
1853

EFFICIENCY   0.1%   0.1%   0.1%   0.1%

LIGHT SOURCES

Light sources turn other kinds of energy into visible radiation. The sun uses nuclear energy. Torches, candles, gas lamps, and other flames use chemical energy. Most of our modern light sources use electrical energy. In the process of making light, most sources waste much energy in the form of heat. Flames are very inefficient, but for many centuries they were the only controlled sources of light. The invention of the Welsbach mantle, in 1866, increased greatly the light output of the common gas lamp. The mantle, a small white wicklike cover placed over the gas flame, is made of thorium oxide to which a little cerium has been added. When heated, it emits visible light but not infrared radiation. Unable to lose energy by infrared emission as do most hot objects, its temperature rises to almost the temperature of the flame, and the mantle gives off a brilliant white light. If a black body (the most efficient radiator) were placed in the same flame, it would lose so much energy by infrared emission that it would remain relatively cool, giving off much less light than the Welsbach mantle.

Carbon arc lamps (high current electrical discharges between carbon electrodes) came into use for public street lighting about 1879. Carbon arcs today are used in powerful searchlights and commercial movie projectors.

In 1879, Thomas Edison invented the incandescent filament lamp which, in much improved form, is still our

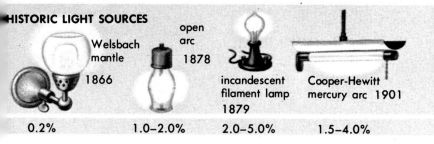

Welsbach mantle 1866	open arc 1878	incandescent filament lamp 1879	Cooper-Hewitt mercury arc 1901
0.2%	1.0–2.0%	2.0–5.0%	1.5–4.0%

most common source for home lighting. The glow tube first appeared in 1850 as a laboratory device for the study of electric discharges, but it has since become more familiar in the commercial "neon" sign. The Cooper-Hewitt mercury arc of 1901, another tube using electric discharges, was one of the ancestors of modern fluorescent lamps.

Light from an incandescent lamp is more concentrated than that from a fluorescent lamp and seems brighter, but it is only about one-third as efficient. A carbon arc is less efficient and less convenient than either, but provides a hotter point source and is far brighter.

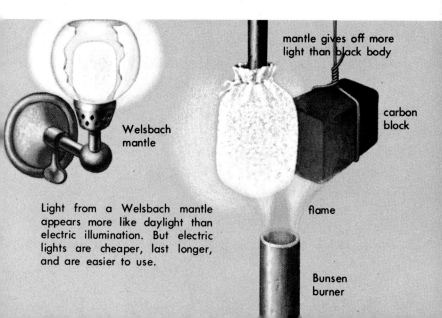

mantle gives off more light than black body

carbon block

Welsbach mantle

flame

Bunsen burner

Light from a Welsbach mantle appears more like daylight than electric illumination. But electric lights are cheaper, last longer, and are easier to use.

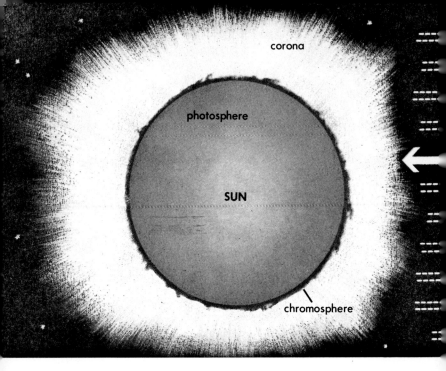

corona

photosphere

SUN

chromosphere

THE SUN, our major light source, gets its energy from nuclear processes in its hot interior, which is estimated to have a temperature of about 13 million degrees K. The sun is a ball of glowing gases that differ from those found on earth because of the sun's extremely high pressures and temperatures. The atoms of the sun's gases are highly ionized; that is, many of the electrons which normally surround the nuclei of the atoms have been stripped away, leaving the atoms . electrically charged. These ionized gases at high pressure emit a continuous spectrum instead of a line spectrum. The wavelength at which we receive the most energy from the sun (the peak of its energy distribution curve) is about 5,400 A. This lies in the green part of the spectrum, close to the wavelength at which the human eye has its greatest sensitivity.

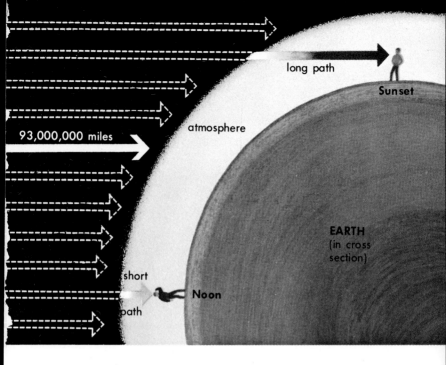

Labels on image: long path, Sunset, 93,000,000 miles, atmosphere, EARTH (in cross section), short, Noon, path

SCATTERING OF SUNLIGHT by the atmosphere is much greater for short (blue) waves than for long (red) ones. When the sun is overhead, the atmospheric path is relatively short, and the sun appears bright yellow, while the scattered light is blue (p. 50). At sunset, the sunlight loses more blue rays by scattering in its longer path through the atmosphere, and the sun appears red. The reflection of this red light from clouds makes the sky pink.

The photosphere, the outer surface of the sun's central core, is the sun's major source of light. Temperature of the photosphere (measured by an optical technique called radiation pyrometry) averages about 5,750°K. Surrounding the photosphere is the chromosphere, composed of cooler gases that absorb some of the photosphere's radiation. This causes dark lines, called Fraunhofer lines (pp. 12–13), in the continuous spectrum of the sun. From measurements of these lines, gases of the chromosphere can be identified.

21

INCANDESCENT LAMPS, the most familiar man-made light sources, consist of a coiled filament of tungsten wire sealed in a glass bulb filled with a mixture of argon and nitrogen gases. Passing an electric current through the filament heats it to a temperature of about 2,900°K. The inert gases surrounding the filament prevent it from burning up and prolong its life by retarding its evaporation.

The energy distribution of the light from an incandescent lamp depends on the filament temperature, so the light tends to be redder than sunlight (5,750°K). In fact, most of the radiation from a tungsten lamp lies in the infrared part of the spectrum. Over 95 per cent of the energy is radiated as heat and less than 5 per cent as light. In spite of this wasted heat energy, the modern light bulb is nearly 10 times as efficient as the first commercial carbon filament lamps. The early clear-glass bulbs have been replaced with bulbs of frosted or translucent glass, often tinted. These newer bulbs provide pleasanter illumination by diffusing the light and softening shadows.

Spectral energy distribution of radiation from tungsten lamp at 3,000° Kelvin. Note how little energy is in the visual range.

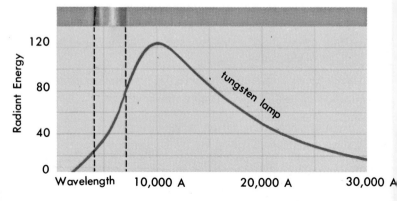

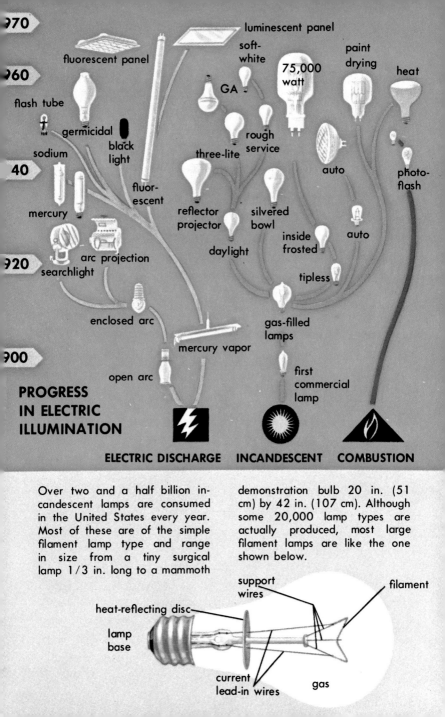

PROGRESS IN ELECTRIC ILLUMINATION

970

960

40

920

900

luminescent panel

fluorescent panel

soft-white

paint drying

heat

flash tube

75,000 watt

GA

germicidal

black light

rough service

sodium

three-lite

mercury

fluor-escent

reflector projector

silvered bowl

auto

photo-flash

daylight

inside frosted

auto

arc projection

searchlight

tipless

enclosed arc

mercury vapor

gas-filled lamps

open arc

first commercial lamp

ELECTRIC DISCHARGE   **INCANDESCENT**   **COMBUSTION**

Over two and a half billion incandescent lamps are consumed in the United States every year. Most of these are of the simple filament lamp type and range in size from a tiny surgical lamp 1/3 in. long to a mammoth demonstration bulb 20 in. (51 cm) by 42 in. (107 cm). Although some 20,000 lamp types are actually produced, most large filament lamps are like the one shown below.

support wires

filament

heat-reflecting disc

lamp base

current lead-in wires

gas

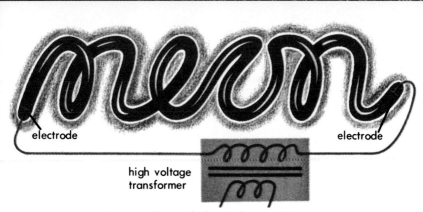

electrode

electrode

high voltage
transformer

A neon sign and electrical connections

GLOW TUBES have many uses in scientific laboratories but are best known as commercial neon signs. These thin tubes have metal electrodes sealed into each end. The air is pumped out of the tube which is then filled with neon or another gas at low pressure.

When a high voltage (1,000–15,000 volts) is applied to the electrodes, stray electrons in the tube are accelerated to high speeds. These collide with the gas atoms, knocking out other electrons, which in turn strike more atoms. This cascading of electrons (shown at right) becomes the electric current that flows through the tube. The fast-moving electrons transfer energy when they collide with neutral gas atoms. The collision may ionize the atom by knocking out one of its electrons (1), or excite the atom by moving an electron to a position of higher energy in the atom (2). Energy is emitted as a light photon when the atom returns to its normal state (3). When a free electron is captured by an ionized atom (4) it gives up its energy as a photon. Photons are units of light energy that act like particles. The energy of each photon depends on its frequency. The frequency of the emitted photon is proportional to the energy lost by the electron in falling to a lower energy state or the energy given up by the electron captured by the ionized atom.

Each kind of atom when excited gives off light at frequencies determined by its structure. Some gases emit light only at a few wavelengths. The spectrum of sodium, for example, shows two bright yellow lines very close together, and a sodium vapor lamp gives out a yellow light since the brightest lines in the spectrum determine the color of the light from the glow tube. Sodium vapor lamps are used in street lighting. Neon tubes glow an orange-red. Tubes filled with krypton give a pale blue light. Other gases or mixtures of gases are often used, sometimes in tinted or fluorescent glass tubes which modify the color of the light.

CASCADE REACTION

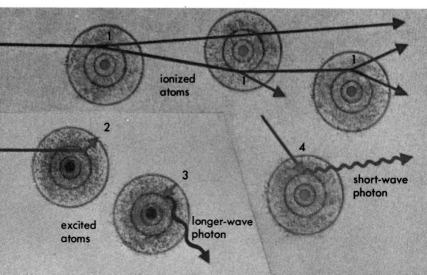

ionized atoms

excited atoms

longer-wave photon

short-wave photon

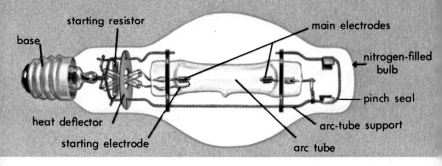

Labels: base, starting resistor, main electrodes, nitrogen-filled bulb, pinch seal, arc-tube support, heat deflector, starting electrode, arc tube

This high-pressure lamp contains an arc tube within a nitrogen-filled bulb.

THE MERCURY ARC is very much like a glow tube, but uses higher current so that the electrode operates at a red heat. If the pressure of the mercury vapor in the tube is high (from 1/100 atmosphere to several hundred atmospheres), the arc will give off an intense bluish-white light as well as some ultraviolet. If the pressure is low (from about 1/100,000 to 1/1,000 of atmospheric pressure), most of the radiation will be in the ultraviolet. Sunlamps are usually low-pressure mercury arcs enclosed in bulbs of fused quartz. High-pressure lamps are frequently used for street lighting or for making blueprints.

FLUORESCENT LAMPS use a low-pressure mercury arc within a glass tube coated on the inside with a phosphor such as calcium tungstate. Phosphors have the ability to absorb ultraviolet rays and to re-radiate the energy as light. The spectrum emitted by a fluorescent tube depends largely on the mixture of fluorescent chemicals used in the phosphor coating. A careful selection of phosphors will produce radiation with broad bands in the visible region of the spectrum, and very little in the ultraviolet or infrared. Proper phosphors can approximate the color of sunlight without high temperatures.

A FLUORESCENT TUBE

(cross section) glows when ultra-violet rays excite the electrons of the phosphor coating. As these excited electrons drop back to lower energy levels, light is emitted. The color of the light depends on the structure of the phosphor.

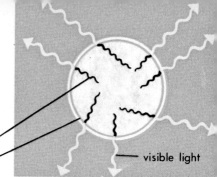

ultraviolet light
phosphor coating
visible light

THE SPECTRUM of a fluorescent lamp, combining light from phosphor and mercury, approximates that of sunlight.

RAPID-START fluorescent circuits are more efficient. A ballast in the circuit eliminates flicker.

▼

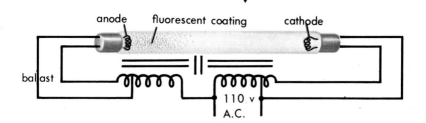

anode   fluorescent coating   cathode

ballast

110 v
A.C.

SPECTRAL ENERGY CURVE

Compare the spectral energy curve of a 40-watt "daylight" fluorescent lamp with those of the average daylight curve and of a tungsten lamp curve (p. 22).

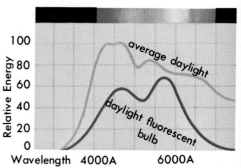

average daylight

daylight fluorescent bulb

Relative Energy
100
80
60
40
20
0

Wavelength   4000A   6000A

27

LUMINESCENCE, or the emission of light, may be due to causes other than heat (thermoluminescence).

CHEMILUMINESCENCE is the emission of light during a chemical reaction. When a formaldehyde solution is mixed into an alkaline alcohol solution, chemical energy is changed into light, causing the mixture to glow.

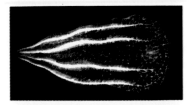

BIOLUMINESCENCE is the production of light by chemiluminescence in living organisms, as in certain fungi, bacteria, comb jellyfish (left), fireflies, and fishes. The Railroad Worm, a beetle larva, is bioluminescent in two colors.

FLUORESCENCE is the production of light when a substance is exposed to ultraviolet or other radiation (including beams of electrons or other particles). Most cases of fluorescence are really examples of phosphorescence.

PHOSPHORESCENCE is delayed fluorescence. The light emission continues for a time after the exciting radiation stops. Television tubes have a phosphorescent coating and thus produce pictures without apparent flicker.

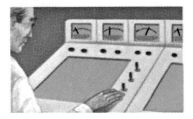

ELECTROLUMINESCENCE offers a new source of diffuse illumination for lighting. Alternating current applied to thin conducting panels excites luminescent material sandwiched between them, producing a soft, easily regulated glow.

ILLUMINATION

Illumination is often used as a general term that refers to the quantity and quality of light. The illumination of a scene may be bright or dim, harsh or soft, and perhaps even cold or warm. These terms refer loosely to the amount, contrast, and hue (color) of the light. In a narrower sense, illuminance is the amount of light received on a specified surface area.

The range of sensitivity of your eyes to light is so great that you are able to see clearly under widely different conditions of illumination. The ratio of the illuminance at noonday to that on a moonless night may be as great as ten million to one. On a clear day there may be 20 times as much illumination on the sunny side of a building as on the shaded side. Modern indoor lighting for houses calls for illumination that is about one fifth that found on the shaded side of a building on a clear day. This is 20 times more illumination than was once considered adequate for homes. Improved illumination greatly increases the ease with which reading or fine work can be done.

The human eye cannot distinguish the component wavelengths of a light beam, nor can it detect small changes in spectral distribution. Neither is the eye equally sensitive to all wavelengths. Measurements made with many people have produced a standard luminosity curve (p. 30) that represents the relative sensitivity of the average eye to different wavelengths of light.

Radiant energy, including light, is a physical quantity that can be measured directly by several types of radiation detectors, such as thermopiles, bolometers, and wave meters. Visible light can be measured by a photometer or a light meter.

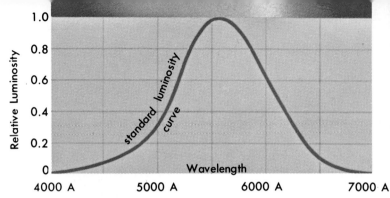

Relative Luminosity

1.0
0.8
0.6
0.4
0.2
0

standard luminosity curve

Wavelength

4000 A   5000 A   6000 A   7000 A

LUMINOSITY is the ability of light to excite the sensation of brightness (p. 32). The standard lumi- nosity curve peaks at 5,550 A, indicating that our eyes are most sensitive to yellow-green light.

VARIATIONS IN

ARTIFICIAL LIGHT indoors is very different from outdoor light, yet you rarely notice that your green sweater is of a somewhat different color as you come indoors. Just as your eyes adapt to changes in light intensity, so they adapt to changes in light quality. Color photographs show the difference because, unlike your eyes, the film cannot adapt its sensitivity to the changed illumination. Film designed for indoor use with incandescent lamps produces a very bluish or cold picture if used outdoors. Film designed for outdoor use results in a very orange or warm picture when used with artificial light indoors.

Outdoor film, outdoor light

Outdoor film, indoor light
Indoor film, outdoor light

Indoor film, indoor light

Dawn

↑ Midmorning

Noon

ILLUMINATION

DAYLIGHT changes color constantly from sunrise to sunset. A color photograph taken in early morning or in late afternoon will have much warmer colors than one taken when the sun is overhead. Color film properly records the differences in the color of daylight, but human vision simply compensates for the differences. You notice only extreme changes in the color of daylight, as at sunrise or sunset.

↓ Late afternoon

Midafternoon

BRIGHTNESS is a purely psychological concept. It is a sensation of the observer and cannot be measured by instruments. The ability of the eye to judge absolute values of brightness is very poor due to its great powers of adaptation. The eye is a very sensitive detector of brightness differences, however, provided the two fields of view are presented simultaneously. The measurement of light by visual comparison is the basis of the science of photometry.

Light-source intensity depends on the total amount of light emitted and on the smallness of the conical solid angle in which it is emitted. Stated simply, it is the amount of light emitted in a given direction.

Brightness is associated with the amount of the light stimulus. It is the visual sensation corresponding to the perception of luminance. Luminance, the intensity of light-source per unit area, is a psychophysical property and can be measured. Luminance and light-source intensity, often confused, are best described by examples.

THE TWO LUMINOUS SPHERES of different size (below left) have identical light bulbs. They are diffuse emitters and so will appear as luminous discs from any viewpoint. Both emit the same total amount of light, and both have the same intensity. But the smaller one will appear brighter to the observer and will have the higher luminance.

In order for the two spheres to have the same luminance the larger sphere would require a larger (more intense) light source (below right). It would then emit the same amount of light per unit area of surface as does the smaller sphere. The two spheres would then appear equally bright, but the larger one would have the greater intensity.

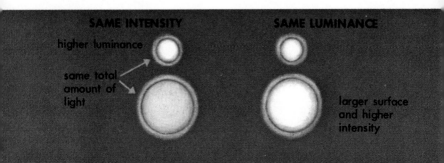

SAME INTENSITY   SAME LUMINANCE

higher luminance

same total
amount of
light

larger surface
and higher
intensity

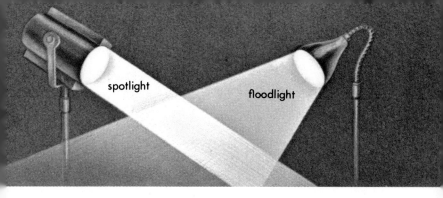

spotlight

floodlight

THE RELATIONSHIP OF INTENSITY to conical angle is shown by comparing a spotlight and a floodlight with identical light bulbs in reflectors of the same diameter but dissimilar shape (above). The spotlight beam is concentrated into a small cone with rays almost parallel. The floodlight, which emits the same amount of light, spreads it into a large cone. The spotlight provides a much greater illuminance but over a much smaller area than the floodlight.

If we look directly into the beam of the light source, the spotlight appears to be much brighter than the floodlight. In that direction only, the intensity and the luminance of the spotlight are greater than those of the floodlight. If we look at the light source from other directions outside the beam, the intensity and luminance of the spotlight are much less, because so much light is concentrated into the beam that there is little left to go in these other directions.

PHOTOMETRIC UNITS are used in the quantitative measurement of illumination. A few of the more important ones are given below for reference.

LUMINOUS FLUX is the quantity of light. It is measured in lumens. Intensity is luminous flux per unit solid angle. It is measured in candles. (1 candle = 1 lumen per unit solid angle.) Illuminance is incident flux per unit area. It is measured in lux. (1 lux = 1 lumen per meter^2.) Luminance is intensity per unit area. It is measured in candles per meter^2.

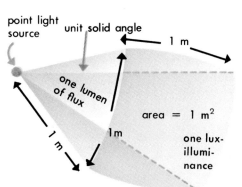

point light source

unit solid angle

1 m

one lumen of flux

1m

1 m

area = 1 m^2

one lux-illuminance

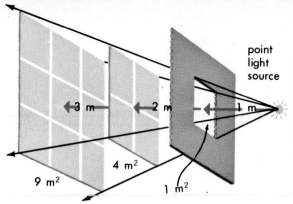

Light that illuminates a one-square-meter surface at one meter will cover four square meters at two meters and spreads over nine square meters at three meters.

A POINT LIGHT SOURCE radiates its energy uniformly so that light rays spread out from it in all directions. Illumination at a point on a surface varies with the intensity and shape of the light source and the distance of the surface from it. The amount of light falling on a unit area (the illuminance) decreases with the square of the distance (the inverse square law).

SHADOWS are formed when light cannot pass through an opaque body in its path. Illumination of the area behind the body is cut off. A small (pinpoint) or distant source of light casts a sharp shadow. A near, large, or diffuse light source produces a fuzzy shadow with a central dark area that receives no light (umbra) and a light outer area (penumbra) which receives some light from part of the source.

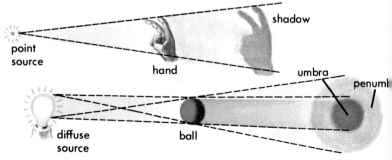

LIGHTNESS is a term used by an observer to distinguish between lightness and darkness of colored objects, as between light blue and dark blue paint. It should not be confused with brightness (p. 32). The observer's perception of lightness is also a recognition of a difference in whiteness or grayness between objects. It is a comparative term referring to the amount of diffusely reflected light coming to the observer's eye from a surface. The surface will appear white if it is a good non-selective diffuse reflector and is well illuminated by white light. If it is a poor reflector or if it receives little or no illumination, the surface will appear gray, grayer, or even black. Black, then, is the perception of an area from which the light is insufficient for detailed vision. White is the perception of a well-illuminated surface whose reflectance is high and non-selective. Gray is the perception of a surface between these extremes.

THE PERCEPTION OF GRAYNESS is influenced by, among other things, the illumination of the surrounding area. The gray areas at the bottom of the page are identical, but the one surrounded by black appears to be much lighter than the one surrounded by white. Because of the amount of light reflected, the three areas below are seen as black, gray, and white.

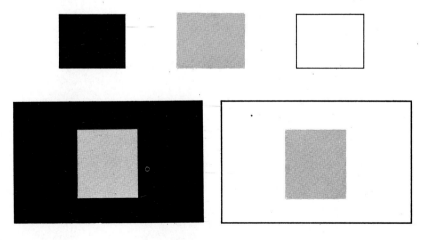

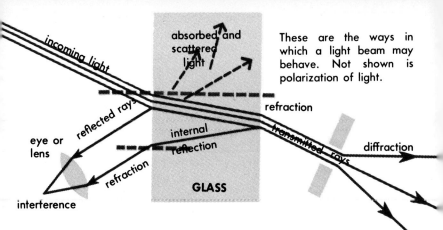

absorbed and scattered light

These are the ways in which a light beam may behave. Not shown is polarization of light.

incoming light

refraction

reflected rays

internal reflection

transmitted rays

diffraction

eye or lens

refraction

GLASS

interference

LIGHT BEHAVIOR

Light behavior includes transmission, absorption, reflection, refraction, scattering, diffraction, interference and polarization, all of which are discussed in this section. Transmission, absorption and reflection account for all the light energy when light strikes an object. In the course of transmission, light may be scattered, refracted or polarized. It can also be polarized by reflection. The light that is not transmitted or reflected is absorbed and its energy contributes to the heat energy of the molecules of the absorbing material. The modification of light through these processes is responsible for all that we see.

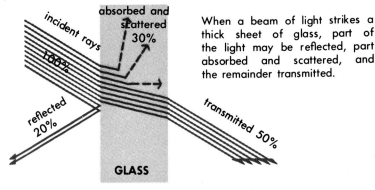

incident rays

absorbed and scattered 30%

100%

When a beam of light strikes a thick sheet of glass, part of the light may be reflected, part absorbed and scattered, and the remainder transmitted.

reflected 20%

transmitted 50%

GLASS

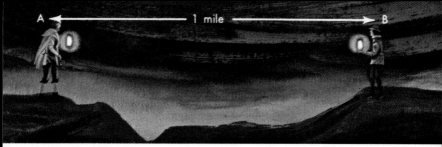

A ◄———— 1 mile ————► B

LIGHT TRAVELS so fast that for many years scientists thought that its speed was infinite. The first observations and measurements which gave a finite value to the speed of light were made by the Danish astronomer Olaf Roemer in 1675. Roemer was measuring the period of revolution of one of Jupiter's satellites by timing its successive eclipses behind the planet. He found that the measurements made while the earth was receding from Jupiter gave longer periods than those made while the earth was approaching Jupiter. Roemer concluded that the difference was due to the fact that in the receding position the light from each successive eclipse had to travel a greater distance to reach the earth and therefore took a longer time (diagram, p. 38). He calculated that light took about 22 minutes to travel a distance equal to the diameter of the earth's orbit about the sun. Roemer's method was correct but his accuracy was poor. We now know that the time required is nearly 16.67 minutes, or about 1,000 seconds. Since the diameter of the earth's orbit is about 186,000,000 miles, the speed of light is calculated to be about 186,000 miles per second.

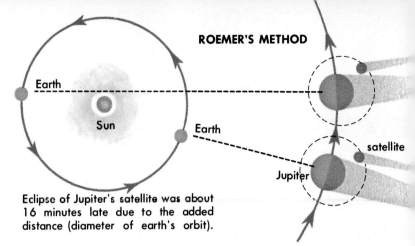

ROEMER'S METHOD

Earth

Sun

Earth

satellite

Jupiter

Eclipse of Jupiter's satellite was about 16 minutes late due to the added distance (diameter of earth's orbit).

MODERN MEASUREMENTS of the speed of light are made in the laboratory. Using many different techniques and much elaborate apparatus, scientists have measured the speed of light in free space again and again, always striving for more accuracy. The value now accepted is 299,793 kilometers, or 186,282 miles, per second. The error is believed to be less than one thousandth of one per cent. The precise measurement of the speed of light, a fundamental constant, is one of the great technical achievements of our time.

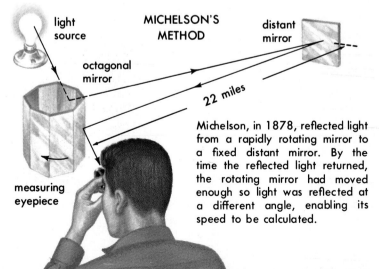

light source

MICHELSON'S METHOD

distant mirror

octagonal mirror

22 miles

measuring eyepiece

Michelson, in 1878, reflected light from a rapidly rotating mirror to a fixed distant mirror. By the time the reflected light returned, the rotating mirror had moved enough so light was reflected at a different angle, enabling its speed to be calculated.

REFLECTION is of two kinds—diffuse and regular. Diffuse reflection is the kind by which we ordinarily see objects. It gives us information about their shape, size, color and texture. Regular reflection is mirrorlike. We don't see the surface of the mirror; instead, we see objects that are reflected in it. When light strikes a mirror at an angle, it is reflected at the same angle. In diffuse reflection, light leaves at many different angles. The degree of surface roughness determines the proportion of diffuse and regular reflection that occurs. Reflection from a smooth, polished surface like a mirror is mostly regular, while diffuse reflection takes place at surfaces that are rough compared with the wavelength of light. Since the wavelength of light is very small (about 5,000 A), most reflection is diffuse.

VIEWED MICROSCOPICALLY, all reflection is regular. The appearance of diffuse reflection is due to the many different angles that light rays encounter when they strike a rough surface. The reflection of each single ray is regular—that is, it is reflected at the same angle at which it strikes the surface. A fairly smooth surface, such as that of a glossy vinyl raincoat, shows both diffuse and regular reflection, the relative proportions depending on the angle of the incident light. But a rough surface, such as that of a tweed coat, shows only diffuse reflection. It has no "shiny" surface.

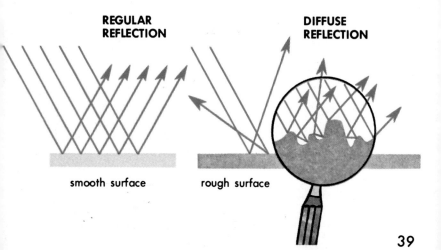

REGULAR REFLECTION

smooth surface

DIFFUSE REFLECTION

rough surface

REFLECTION VARIES with the type of material. Polished metal reflects most of the light that falls on it, absorbs only a little, and transmits practically none. Paper is made up of partly transparent fibers. Light striking paper may penetrate several fibers, being partly reflected at each surface. The light that finally reaches your eyes and lets you know you are looking at paper has been reflected and transmitted many times. All the rest of the light has been absorbed and added to the heat energy of the molecules of the paper.

Most materials are quite selective in the way they absorb and reflect the different wavelengths of light. A purple dye will transmit blue and red light but will absorb green light. Gold and copper metals reflect red and yellow wavelengths more strongly than blue. Silver reflects all colors and therefore appears almost white. Metallic reflection is an example of pure surface color. Nearly all "object colors" are due to selective reflection and absorption of light. Object colors are an attribute of the object, though the color seen at any time depends also on the color of the illumination. Total absorption of light makes an object look black.

incident rays

woven material

diffuse reflection

REFLECTED LIGHT reveals the color and texture of woven cloth. What we normally consider as reflection involves selective absorption, selective reflection and refraction of light that partially penetrates the surface.

enlarged cross section of fibers

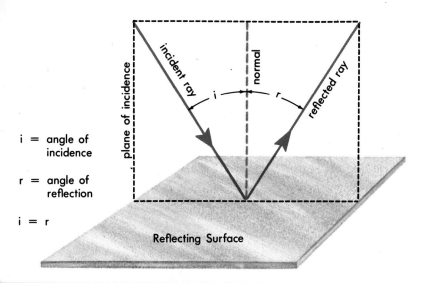

i = angle of incidence

r = angle of reflection

i = r

Reflecting Surface

LAWS OF REFLECTION

1. Angle of reflection equals angle of incidence.
2. Incident and reflected rays lie in the same plane.
3. Incident and reflected rays are on opposite sides of the normal—a line perpendicular to the reflecting surface and passing through the point of incidence.

A PLANE MIRROR reverses a scene from left to right. Objects held in the left hand of a subject appear to be in the right hand of the image. All objects seen in the mirror appear to be as far behind the surface as they actually are in front of it.

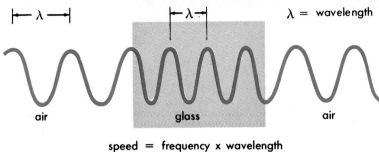

$$\text{speed} = \text{frequency} \times \text{wavelength}$$

$$\text{refractive index of glass} = \frac{\text{speed in air}}{\text{speed in glass}} = \frac{\text{wavelength in air}}{\text{wavelength in glass}}$$

REFRACTION is the bending of a light ray when it crosses the boundary between two different materials, as from air into water. This change in direction is due to a change in speed. Light travels fastest in empty space and slows down upon entering matter. Its speed in air is almost the same as its speed in space, but it travels only ¾ as fast in water and only ⅔ as fast in glass. The refractive index of a substance is the ratio of the speed of light in space (or in air) to its speed in the substance. This ratio is always greater than one.

When a beam of light enters a pane of glass perpendicular to the surface (above), it slows down, and its wavelength in the glass becomes shorter in the same proportion. The frequency remains the same. Coming out of the glass, the light speeds up again, the wavelength returning to its former size.

When a light ray strikes the glass at some other angle, it changes direction as well as speed. Inside the glass, the ray bends toward the perpendicular or normal. If the two sides of the glass are parallel, the light will return to its original direction when it leaves the glass, even though it has been displaced in its passage. If the two sides of the glass are not parallel, as in the case of a prism or a lens, the ray emerges in a new direction.

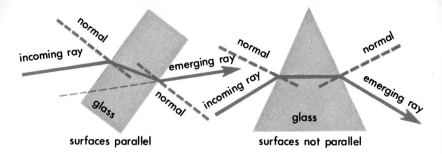

surfaces parallel   surfaces not parallel

LAWS OF REFRACTION

1. Incident and refracted rays lie in the same plane.
2. When a ray of light passes at an angle into a denser medium, it is bent toward the normal, hence the angle of refraction (r) is smaller than the angle of incidence (i), as below.
3. The index of refraction of any medium is the ratio between the speed of light in a vacuum (or in air) and its speed in the medium.

THE INDEX OF REFRACTION (n) determines the amount of bending of a light ray as it crosses the boundary from air into the medium. For example, in any of the diagrams below, the ratio between the line x and the line y, $(\frac{x}{y})$, is equal to the refractive index (n) if d is the same length in both air and the medium.

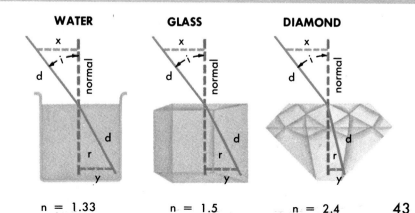

WATER	GLASS	DIAMOND
n = 1.33	n = 1.5	n = 2.4

43

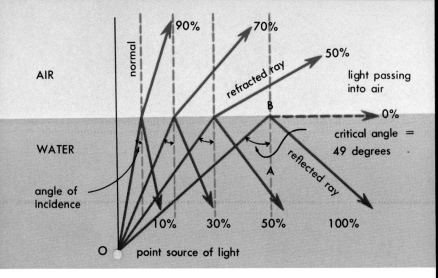

normal

AIR

90%   70%   50%

light passing
into air

refracted ray

B   0%

critical angle =
49 degrees

WATER

reflected ray

A

angle of
incidence

10%   30%   50%   100%

O   point source of light

FROM A POINT SOURCE (O) under water, the refracted rays in air make larger and larger angles with the normal, as the angles of incidence become larger. At the same time, the amount of light reflected back into the water increases. Finally, for the ray OB, when the angle of refraction be- comes 90°, all the light is reflected. The angle of incidence OBA, called the critical angle, for pure water is 49°; for a ray striking a glass-air surface, it is about 40°. Because of this, a 45-90-45° prism reflects 100% of the light entering it and can therefore be used as a perfect mirror (p. 60).

INTERNAL REFLECTION occurs whenever a light ray strikes the surface of a medium whose refractive index is less than that of the medium in which the light is traveling. The amount of light that is reflected depends on the angle at which it hits the surface. Light from a point source (above) hits the surface at many angles.

DISPERSION is the separation of light into its component wavelengths. One method of dispersing a light beam is to pass it through a glass prism—a thick piece of glass with flat non-parallel sides (below). The refractive index of all materials (p. 43) depends slightly on the wavelength of the light. For glass and other transparent materials the refractive index is larger for the short (blue) wavelengths than for the longer (red) ones. Thus, when a beam of white light is passed through a prism, the blue rays will be bent more than the red rays—that is, the light spreads out to form a spectrum. The colors in the spectrum appear in the order of increasing wavelength: violet, blue, green, yellow, orange, and red. Sir Isaac Newton first explained the spectrum. He showed that, contrary to popular belief, the prism did not create the beautiful colors, but only made visible the components of white light.

Scientists make use of dispersion in the analysis of light emitted or absorbed by various materials both on the earth and on other bodies in space (p. 63).

WHITE LIGHT (below) entering through a narrow slit at the left strikes the prism at an acute angle. The longer-wavelength red rays are bent less than the shorter-wavelength blue, so a partial separation occurs in the glass. The beam then strikes the second surface of the prism, again at an acute angle, and the rays are once again refracted. They leave the prism as divergent rays of different wavelengths. A white screen is placed some distance from the prism and the different colors appear on it. The spectrum consists of many images of the slit, each of different color.

DIFFRACTION is the bending of waves around an obstacle. It is easy to see this effect for water waves. They bend around the corner of a sea wall, or spread as they move out of a channel. Diffraction of light waves, however, is harder to observe. In fact, diffraction of light waves is so slight that it escaped notice for a long time. The amount of bending is proportional to the size of light waves—about one fifty-thousandth of an inch (5,000 A)—so the bending is always very small indeed.

When light from a distant street lamp is viewed through a window screen it forms a cross. The four sides of each tiny screen hole act as the sides of a slit and bend light in four directions, producing a cross made of four prongs of light. Another way to see the diffraction of light waves is to look at a distant light bulb through a very narrow vertical slit. Light from the bulb

A PATTERN OF WAVES will move outward, forming concentric circles, if small pebbles are dropped regularly from a fixed point into a quiet pond. If a board is placed in the path of these waves, they will be seen to bend around the edges of the board, causing an interesting pattern where the waves from the two edges of the board meet and cross each other. When an obstruction with a vertical slit is placed in the pond in the path of the waves, the waves spread out in circles beyond the slit.

board

slit

bends at both edges of the slit and appears to spread out sideways, forming an elongated diffraction pattern in a direction perpendicular to the slit.

Light can be imagined as waves whose fronts spread out in expanding concentric spheres around a source. Each point on a wave front can be thought of as the source of a new disturbance. Each point can act as a new light source with a new series of concentric wave fronts expanding outward from it. Points are infinitely numerous on the surface of a wave front as it crosses an opening.

As new wave fronts fan out from each point of a small opening, such as a pinhole or a narrow slit, they reinforce each other when they are in phase (p. 48) and cancel each other when they are completely out of phase. Thus lighter and darker areas form the banded diffraction patterns.

DIFFRACTION PATTERNS are formed when light from a point source passes through pinholes and slits. A pinhole gives a circular pattern and a slit gives an elongated pattern. A sharp image is not formed by light passing through because of diffraction.

As the pinhole or slit gets smaller, the diffraction pattern gets larger but dimmer. In the diffraction patterns shown below the alternate light and dark spaces are due to interference (p. 48) between waves arriving from different parts of the pinhole or slit.

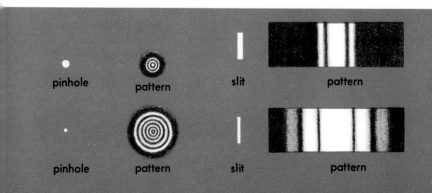

pinhole   pattern   slit   pattern

pinhole   pattern   slit   pattern

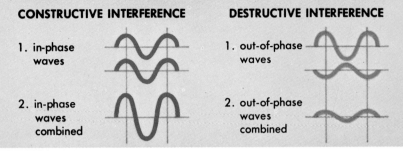

CONSTRUCTIVE INTERFERENCE

1. in-phase waves

2. in-phase waves combined

DESTRUCTIVE INTERFERENCE

1. out-of-phase waves

2. out-of-phase waves combined

INTERFERENCE is an effect that occurs when two waves of equal frequency are superimposed. This often happens when light rays from a single source travel by different paths to the same point. If, at the point of meeting, the two waves are in phase (vibrating in unison, and the crest of one coinciding with the crest of the other), they will combine to form a new wave of the same frequency. The amplitude of the new wave is the sum of the amplitudes of the original waves. The process of forming this new wave is called constructive interference.

If the two waves meet out of phase (crest of one coinciding with a trough of the other), the result is a wave whose amplitude is the difference of the original amplitudes. This process is called destructive interference. If the original waves have equal amplitudes,

INTERFERENCE OCCURS when light waves from a point source (a single slit) travel by two different paths (through the double slit). Their interference is shown by a pattern of alternate light and dark bands when a screen is placed across their path.

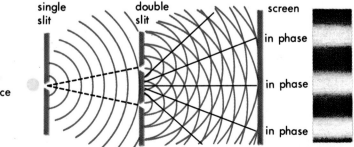

48

they may completely destroy each other, leaving no wave at all. Constructive interference results in a bright spot; destructive interference produces a dark spot.

Partial constructive or destructive interference results whenever the waves have an intermediate phase relationship. Interference of waves does not create or destroy light energy, but merely redistributes it.

Two waves interfere only if their phase relationship does not change. They are then said to be coherent. Light waves from two different sources do not interfere because radiations from different atoms are constantly changing their phase relationships. They are non-coherent (see lasers, p. 152.)

IRIDESCENT COLORS, which change their appearance with the angle of viewing and the direction of the illumination, are due to interference. The delicate hues of soap bubbles and oil films, the pale tints of mother-of-pearl, and the brilliant colors of a peacock's tail are all iridescent colors.

A SOAP BUBBLE appears iridescent under white light when the thickness of the bubble is of the order of a wavelength of light. This occurs because light waves reflected from front and back surfaces of the film travel different distances. A difference in phase results that may cause destructive interference for some particular wavelength, and the hue or color associated with that wavelength will be absent from the reflected light. If the missing hue is red, reflected light appears blue-green, the complement of red. If film thickness or direction of illumination changes, interference occurs at different wavelengths and the reflected light changes color.

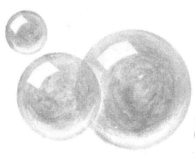

red reflections
cancel if film
thickness is
one-half
wavelength
of red

film of soap bubble
(highly enlarged)

When a beam of white light passes through milk, the blue components are scattered, the reds are transmitted.

diluted milk

SCATTERING is the random deflection of light rays by fine particles. When sunlight enters through a crack, scattering by dust particles in the air makes the shaft of light visible. Haze is a result of light scattering by fog and smoke particles.

Reflection, diffraction, and interference all play a part in the complex phenomenon of scattering. If the scattering particles are of uniform size and much smaller than the wavelength of light, selective scattering may occur and the material will appear colored, as shown above. Shorter wavelengths will be scattered much more strongly than longer ones. In general, scattered light will appear bluish, while the remaining directly transmitted light will lack the scattered blue rays and thus appear orange or red. Many natural blue tints are due to selective scattering rather than to blue pigments. The blue of skies and oceans is due to this kind of scattering. Blue eyes are the result of light scattering in the iris when a dark pigment is lacking.

Scattering by larger particles is nonselective and produces white. The whiteness of a bird's feather, of snow, and of clouds—all are due to scattering by particles which, though small, are large compared to the wavelength of light.

ABSORPTION AND TRANSMISSION BY OPTICAL MATERIALS

ultra-violet	vis-ible	infrared			
0		10,000 A	20,000 A	30,000 A	40,000 A

crown glass

flint glass

quartz

rock salt   to 145,000 A

Since crown glass and flint glass absorb ultraviolet light, a quartz bulb is used for the light source of a sun lamp.

ABSORPTION of light as it passes through matter results in a decrease in intensity. Absorption, like scattering (p. 50), may be general or selective. Selective absorption gives the world most of the colors we see. Glass filters which absorb part of the visible spectrum are used in research and photography. An absorption curve for a filter (below) shows the amount of light absorbed at a particular wavelength. A unit thickness of the absorbing medium will always absorb the same fraction of light from a beam. If the first millimeter thickness of a filter absorbs ½ the light, the second millimeter absorbs ½ the remaining light, or ¼ of the total. The third millimeter absorbs ½ of the ¼, so only ⅛ of the light is transmitted through three millimeters of filter. See also p. 111.

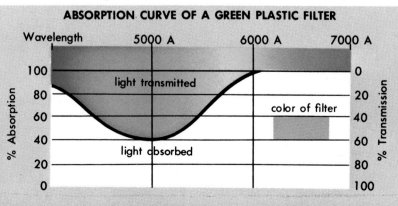

ABSORPTION CURVE OF A GREEN PLASTIC FILTER

Wavelength   5000 A   6000 A   7000 A

% Absorption: 100, 80, 60, 40, 20, 0

% Transmission: 0, 20, 40, 60, 80, 100

light transmitted

light absorbed

color of filter

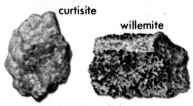

curtisite
willemite
under white light

curtisite
willemite
under ultraviolet

FLUORESCENT MINERALS seen under white light (left) emit colored light (right) when exposed to invisible ultraviolet rays. The color of the fluorescence depends on the nature of the mineral.

FLUORESCENCE AND PHOSPHORESCENCE are caused by light striking atoms. In the collision, energy is transferred from the light to the electrons of the atoms. This energy may be re-radiated as light or dissipated as heat. If the emitted light is of the same frequency as the incident light, the effect is a kind of scattering. In many cases, however, the emitted light is of a different (usually lower) frequency than the incident light, and is characteristic of the atom that emitted it. The immediate re-radiation of absorbed light energy as light of a different color is called fluorescence.

Some materials continue to emit light for a time after the incident radiation has been cut off. This is phosphorescence, usually a property of crystals or of large organic molecules. Phosphorescence often depends on the presence of minute quantities of impurities or imperfections in the crystal that provide "traps" for excited electrons. These electrons have received extra energy from incident radiation. The electrons remain in the "traps" until shaken loose by the heat vibrations of the atoms in the crystal. Phosphorescent light is emitted as the electrons return to their normal positions. Solid substances that produce light in this way are called phosphors.

THIN PLATES OF TOURMALINE transmit light with vibrations restricted to a single plane (polarized light). When one plate is turned so its axis is at right angles to the other, no light passes through. Good natural crystals of tourmaline are rare. Better polarizing materials made synthetically are now available.

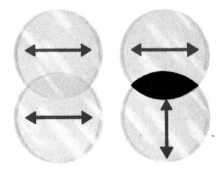

POLARIZED LIGHT waves are restricted in their direction of vibration. Normal light waves vibrate in an infinite number of directions perpendicular to their direction of travel (p. 8). For example, in the head-on view of unpolarized light (below right) the lines a, b, c, d, and an infinite number of others are perpendicular to the ray. At a particular instant any one of them might represent the direction of the vibrations. Thus, from moment to moment, the direction of the light vibrations changes in a random fashion. When components of vibration in one direction only are present, the light is plane polarized.

CONCEPTUAL ERRORS may be introduced when illustrating polarized light. Of the various possibilities, the symbols used below give the best analogy to the events happening with polarization.

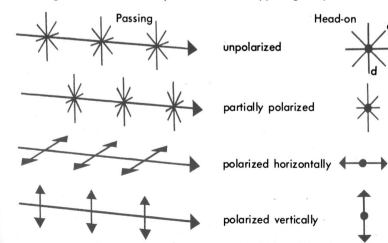

Passing

unpolarized

partially polarized

polarized horizontally

polarized vertically

Head-on

53

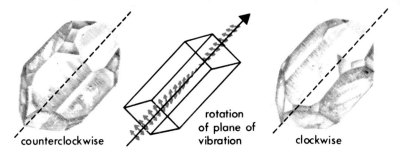

counterclockwise

rotation
of plane of
vibration

clockwise

THE PLANE OF VIBRATION of a polarized light wave is usually unaffected in passing through a transparent material—it remains polarized in the same plane. Some optically active materials, however, rotate the plane of vibration in either a clockwise or counterclockwise direction. Quartz crystals occur in both clockwise and counterclockwise varieties. Sugar solutions are also optically active. A chemist can determine the concentration of sugar in a solution by measuring the rotation of the plane of vibration when plane-polarized light is passed through the solution. A dextrose sugar solution causes a clockwise rotation; levulose sugar, a counterclockwise one. A device for measuring the angle of rotation of the plane of vibration is called a polariscope. A saccharimeter is a polariscope used in sugar analyses.

a vertically polarized ray

may be rotated clockwise
or counterclockwise

Polarimeter—
Saccharimeter

Rudolph
Instruments
Engineering Co.

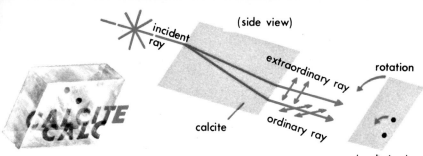

incident ray

extraordinary ray

rotation

calcite

ordinary ray

(end view)

DOUBLY REFRACTING CRYSTALS, such as calcite and quartz, break up light rays into two parts, called ordinary and extraordinary rays, which are polarized at right angles to each other. Such a crystal has a different refractive index for each of the two rays, and they are bent at different angles when they enter the crystal. This double refraction will form two images when a calcite crystal is placed over a dot on a piece of paper. The dot appears as two dots a small distance apart. Rotating the crystal causes one of the dots to rotate about the other. The dot that remains stationary is the image formed by the ordinary ray. This always lies in the plane of incidence (plane including the normal and the incident ray). The moving dot is the image formed by the extraordinary ray.

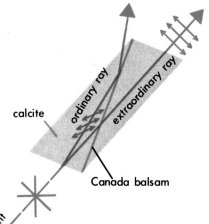

A NICOL PRISM is made by accurately cutting a calcite crystal and cementing the parts back together with Canada balsam. Because of the difference in the refractive indices, the ordinary ray is reflected out the side of the prism by the Canada balsam layer, while the extraordinary ray passes directly through. Nicol prisms were used to produce polarized light rays over a hundred years before the discovery of Polaroid. They are still among the most efficient polarizing devices.

ordinary ray

extraordinary ray

calcite

Canada balsam

incident ray

Without Polaroid filter   With Polaroid filter

POLAROID, invented by Edwin Land in 1932, acts upon light in the same way as tourmaline (p. 53), transmitting only those components of light that are vibrating in one direction. The other components of the wave are absorbed. Polaroid is convenient to use. Polaroid sunglasses, for example, transmit only vertical vibrations, and thus eliminate the glare of light polarized by reflection from horizontal surfaces. Photographers often use Polaroid filters (above) to reduce unwanted reflections, and also to darken the sky in color photographs by removing some of the scattered light, which is partly polarized.

STRESSES in structural parts may be studied in plastic or glass models by placing them between sheets of Polaroid and photographing them under stress. The resulting strains make the plastic or glass doubly refracting (p. 55), but to a different degree for different wavelengths of light. When such material is viewed between Polaroid sheets, beautiful colors appear, indicating the degree of stress.

THREE POLARIZATION PROCESSES are largely responsible for the polarized light that we see. Naturally polarized light is often only partly polarized and effects are not readily noticed.

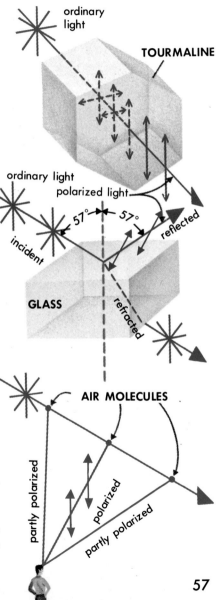

ABSORPTION of light passing through a natural crystal of tourmaline can produce polarization. The crystal resolves all the vibrations of the unpolarized light into two components and absorbs one of them. In one form of Polaroid (p. 56), long, thin molecular chains containing iodine absorb some light vibrations and transmit others.

REFLECTION of light at an angle from a non-metallic surface, such as glass or water, makes it partly polarized. When the reflected ray and refracted ray are at right angles, the reflected ray is completely polarized. In this case, the incident angle is called Brewster's angle. Regularly reflected light (glare) from roads, beaches and water is partly polarized.

SCATTERING partly polarizes light from the sky. Light rays from the sun excite transverse electric vibrations in air molecules, which then scatter polarized light in directions perpendicular to vibrations. Look at the sky 90 degrees away from the sun through a piece of Polaroid. Note change in brightness as the Polaroid is rotated.

57

OPTICAL INSTRUMENTS

An optical instrument uses mirrors, lenses, prisms or gratings, singly or in combination, to reflect, refract or otherwise modify light rays. Optical instruments, especially microscopes and telescopes, have probably broadened man's intellectual horizons more than any other devices he has made.

Perhaps the best way to understand the operation of optical instruments is by geometrical optics—a method that deals with light as rays instead of waves or particles. These rays follow the laws of reflection (p. 41) and refraction (p. 43) as well as the laws of geometry.

IMAGES formed by mirrors and lenses may be either real or virtual and of a predictable size and location. A real image, as formed by a camera or projector, is an actual convening of light rays and can be caught on a screen; virtual images cannot. The rays from object points do not pass through corresponding points of a virtual image. Images seen in binoculars are virtual.

MIRRORS are the oldest and most widely used optical instruments. The plane mirror is the simplest image-forming device. Plane mirrors are found in every home. Spherical or parabolic mirrors are often used in optical instruments instead of lenses.

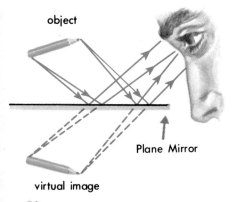

object

Plane Mirror

virtual image

A PLANE OR FLAT MIRROR produces a virtual image since the light rays do not come directly from the image. Rays from an object are redirected by the mirror so that they appear to come from an image located as far behind the mirror as the object is in front of the mirror. Object and image are the same size, but the image is reversed from left to right.

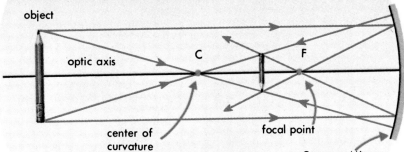

object
optic axis
C
F
center of
curvature
focal point

Concave Mirror

CONCAVE SPHERICAL MIRRORS

have an axis of symmetry through their center, called the optic axis. A point on this axis equidistant from every point on the mirror's surface is the center of curvature. An object beyond the center of curvature forms a real image between the focal point and center of curvature.

1. If a small object is placed at the center of curvature, the mirror forms a real image which coincides with the object but is upside down.

2. As the object is moved closer to the mirror, the image moves rapidly away, getting larger the farther it goes.

3. When the object reaches a point halfway between the mirror and the center of curvature, the reflected rays from each point became parallel and do not form an image at all. The object is then at the focal point of the mirror.

4. If the object is moved closer to the mirror than the focal point, the reflected rays diverge as though they came from a virtual image located behind the mirror. This virtual image is upright and larger than the object.

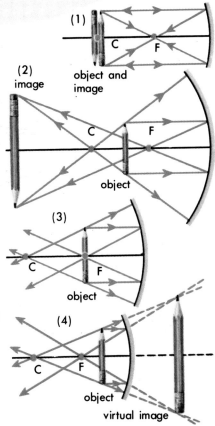

(1) C F
object and image

(2) image C F object

(3) C F object

(4) C F object virtual image

OPTICAL PRISMS are transparent solids of glass or other material whose opposite faces are plane but not necessarily parallel. They are used to bend light rays by refraction or internal reflection. The amount of bending depends on the refractive index of the prism, the angle between its faces, and the angle of incidence of the light. Since the refractive index depends also on the wavelength (p. 45), prisms are often used to disperse a light beam into its spectrum.

45°-90°-45° PRISMS

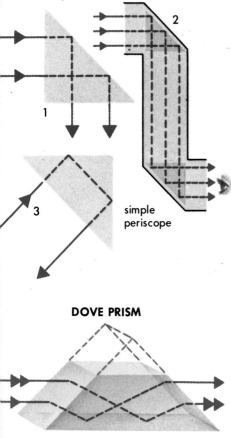

simple periscope

DOVE PRISM

A 45–90–45 DEGREE PRISM will reflect light rays by total internal reflection. When the light rays enter perpendicular to one of the short faces of the prism, they are reflected totally from the long face and depart at right angles to the other short face (1). These prisms are more efficient than silvered mirrors. Two such prisms may be used in periscopes to direct the light down the tube and into the eyepiece (2). The 45–90–45 degree prism may also be turned so that the light rays enter and leave perpendicular to the long face (3). Binoculars (p. 76) use such prisms in this way.

A DOVE PRISM is a modification of the 45–90–45 prism. The 90 degree corner has been removed. The prism interchanges the position of two parallel rays, as shown. If the prism is rotated around the direction of the light, the two rays will rotate about one another at twice the angular speed of the prism rotation. Dove prisms used in optical instruments to invert an image are called erecting prisms.

A TRIPLE MIRROR has the shape of a corner symmetrically sliced from a glass cube. Light entering toward the corner from any direction is reflected back parallel to the direction from which it came. Triple mirrors are used in bicycle and other reflectors, Placed along roads, they reflect the headlights of cars, warning motorists of curves and other changes in driving conditions.

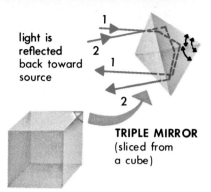

light is reflected back toward source

TRIPLE MIRROR
(sliced from a cube)

A 60–60–60 DEGREE PRISM is used most frequently for dispersing light into its component wavelengths. A new or unknown transparent material is often cut into this shape so its optical properties can be studied with a spectrometer (below), an instrument designed to measure angles of refraction of light rays. In the simplest and most familiar type of spectrometer, light from an outside source enters a narrow, adjustable slit in a collimator tube. It then passes through a lens that renders the rays of light parallel. The rays of light are directed onto a prism that refracts and disperses them in a spectrum that can be viewed through a telescope. The spectrograph (p. 5) is similar in structure but is equipped to photograph the spectra.

SPECTROMETER

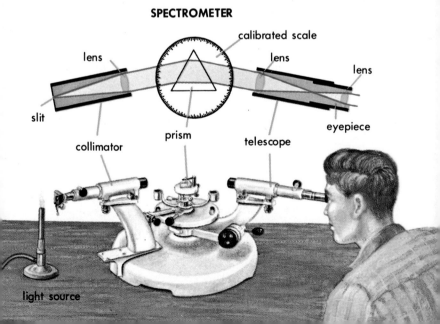

3rd order   2nd order   1st order   central image   1st order   2nd order   3rd order

A diffraction grating produces several orders of the spectrum. The central image is white; higher order spectra overlap.

DIFFRACTION GRATINGS may be used instead of prisms to disperse light. Gratings were first used by Joseph Fraunhofer in 1819 to observe the spectrum of the sun. In 1882 Henry A. Rowland perfected a method of producing gratings of exceptionally high quality. The modern version consists of fine parallel lines (up to 30,000 to the inch) ruled in an aluminum coating on a plane or concave glass surface. Light waves diffracted from these lines interfere so that all wavelengths but one are canceled in any particular direction. Different wavelengths leave the grating at different angles and form a spectrum. Gratings can be used in the ultraviolet and infrared as well as in the visible region of the spectrum; special gratings are used with X-rays.

Dispersion by a prism is greater for short wavelengths than for longer ones. The dispersion of a grating, however, is almost independent of the wavelength. Gratings produce a normal spectrum in which equal distances correspond to equal wavelength intervals and may be superior to a prism in dispersion and resolution.

Gratings produce more than one spectrum at the same time. These occur as a series of ever-wider spectra on either side of a bright central image. The first spectrum on each side is known as a first-order spectrum and is due to interference by a series of waves which are out of phase by one wavelength. The second (second order) spectrum on each side is twice as long (has twice the dispersion) as the first. Each is formed by a series of waves out of phase by two wavelengths. The third order spectrum overlaps the second order spectrum and has three times the dispersion of the first. Higher orders also overlap their neighbors and are longer but dimmer.

Diffraction gratings, like prisms (p. 60), are used in spectroscopes for dispersion of a beam of light. The largest instruments are of the grating type. A spectrograph records the spectrum photographically or electronically. A monochromator, also either prism or grating, uses a slit to isolate a narrow portion of the spectrum for scientific study. These instruments are used to study the many properties of light sources, from candles to distant stars, to learn the kinds of atoms and molecules of which they are made, plus such other features as temperatures, velocities, and energy states. Most of what scientists know about the structure of atoms was learned with spectrographs. The same is true about our knowledge of distant stars, nebulae and galaxies—their temperatures, velocities and chemical structures.

A PASCHEN SPECTROGRAPH uses a concave diffraction grating in a simple manner. The grating, the photographic plate, and the entrance slit are all arranged around a circular track. Light passes through the slit, strikes the grating, and forms spectra of various orders all in focus on the circle. The photographic plate is placed on the track to record desired wavelengths.

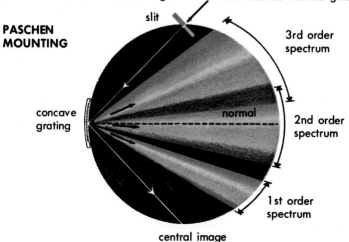

PASCHEN
MOUNTING

slit

3rd order
spectrum

concave
grating

normal

2nd order
spectrum

1st order
spectrum

central image

A LENS forms an image by refracting the light rays from an object. Curved glass lenses were first used as simple magnifiers in the 13th century, but it was not till nearly 1600 that the microscope was devised, followed by the telescope a decade or so later. Mirrors, which form an image by reflecting light rays, had already been known for several centuries and were easier to understand. A lens, however, has an advantage over a mirror in that it permits the observer to be on the opposite side from the incoming light.

SIMPLE POSITIVE LENSES (also known as converging lenses) are single pieces of glass that are thicker at their centers than at their edges. Each surface is a section of a sphere, and a line through the two centers of curvature (AB) is the optic axis. Light passing through a lens is bent toward the thicker part of the glass. Light rays parallel to the optic axis are bent by the lens so as to converge at the focal point (F) of the lens. Similarly, light coming from the opposite direction converges at a second focal point an equal distance on the opposite side of the lens. The distance from the center of the lens (C) to the focal point (F) is the focal length of the lens.

All positive lenses are thicker at their centers than at their edges. They range from very thin lenses with surfaces of little curvature to thick lenses that are nearly spherical in shape. Most lenses in general use are "thin" lenses. Best known and widely used as a simple magnifier is the double convex lens whose surfaces usually, but not always, have the same curvature. The plano-convex lens has one side flat, the other convex. The positive meniscus lens has one convex surface and one concave surface. The convex surface has a smaller radius of curvature than the concave surface. As a result, the lens is always thicker at its center than at its edge.

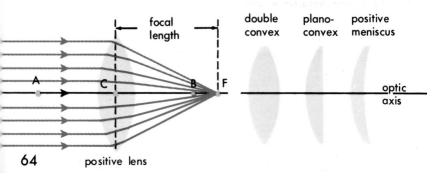

focal length

double convex   plano-convex   positive meniscus

optic axis

positive lens

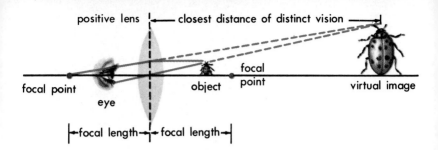

positive lens | closest distance of distinct vision

focal point

eye

object

focal point

virtual image

focal length | focal length

When an object is placed between a positive lens and either focal point, an upright, enlarged image will appear on the same side of the lens but farther away than the object. This virtual image (p. 58) can be seen only by looking at the object through the lens.

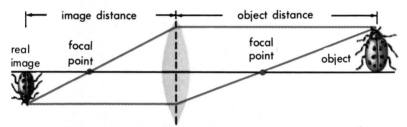

image distance | object distance

real image

focal point

focal point

object

If an object is placed beyond the focal point, its image will be real, inverted, and located on the opposite side of the lens. When the object is more than twice the focal length from the lens the image will be smaller than the object. With the object closer than twice the focal length, the image is larger.

MAGNIFICATION is the ratio of length of image to length of object. It equals the distance of the image divided by the distance of the object from the lens. Hence, an image will be larger than the object only if it is farther from the lens. The shorter the focal length of a lens, or the greater its convex curvature, the greater its magnifying power. This power, expressed in diopters, is the focal length of a lens in meters divided into 1. A lens with a focal length of 25 cm. (¼ m.) has a magnifying power of 4 diopters.

$$\text{magnification} = \frac{\text{image distance}}{\text{object distance}}$$

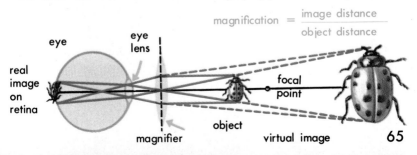

eye

eye lens

real image on retina

focal point

magnifier

object

virtual image

65

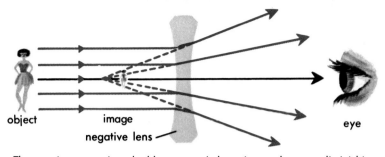

object image negative lens eye

The equiconcave (or double-concave) lens is used as a diminishing glass to see how illustrations will reduce in printing.

SIMPLE NEGATIVE LENSES (also called diverging lenses) are thicker at the edges than at the center. A negative lens alone cannot form a real image as a positive lens does. Light passing through a negative lens parallel to the optic axis is bent away from the axis. The focal point of the negative lens is located by extending these diverging rays backward until they cross the axis. The image formed by a diverging lens is always virtual, upright, and smaller and closer to the lens than the object.

Negative lenses are used to reduce images (below), to correct nearsightedness (p. 69) and to construct compound lenses (p. 71).

Three types of negative lenses

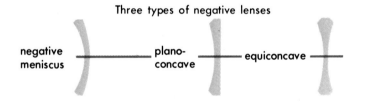

negative meniscus   plano-concave   equiconcave

AN ABERRATION is a failure of a lens or mirror to form a perfect image. Two of the six most important types of aberration are spherical and chromatic. Spherical aberration is caused when parallel light rays passing through a lens at different distances from the optic axis are not all focused at the same point. A diaphragm that decreases the aperture of the lens will eliminate the outer rays and reduce spherical aberration. Chromatic aberration is caused by the fact that a lens bends each color, or wavelength, to a different degree.

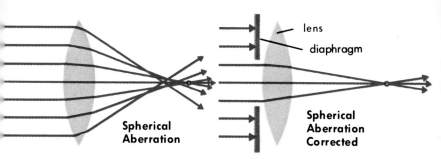

SPHERICAL ABERRATION depends on curvature of the lens. Light rays passing through the outer part of the lens bend too sharply to pass through the focal point and form a fuzzy image.

If the spherical aberration is to be kept to a minimum, the radii of curvature of the lens surfaces should be large compared to the diameter of the lens. A diaphragm limits the lens aperture.

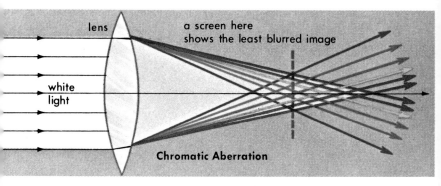

CHROMATIC ABERRATION results from unwanted dispersion of light (p. 45) in a lens, so that different colors are focused at slightly different distances. It produces a blurring of the image in optical instruments.

Chromatic aberration can be corrected by combining two or more simple lenses made of different kinds of glass, so that their dispersions cancel each other. Such lenses are said to be achromatic.

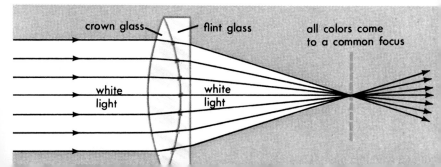

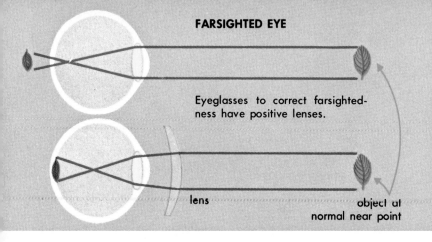

FARSIGHTED EYE

Eyeglasses to correct farsighted-
ness have positive lenses.

lens

object at
normal near point

EYEGLASSES aid a process called accommodation. The muscles attached to the lens of the eye change the shape of the lens so that the images of objects at different distances are brought to a focus on the retina. The range of this accommodation, in normal eyesight, is from a "near point" at which the eye can see an object in most detail (about 10 inches) to a far point on the horizon.

For some people, the near point is much farther away than 10 inches. They see distant objects clearly but are unable to focus on objects at reading distance. Such persons are farsighted (above). The defect in their

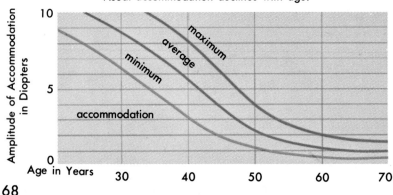

Visual accommodation declines with age.

maximum

average

minimum

accommodation

Amplitude of Accommodation
in Diopters

Age in Years

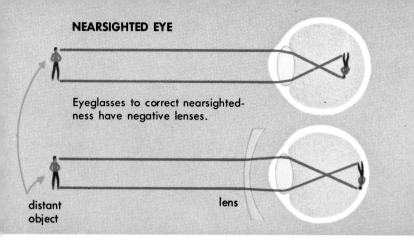

NEARSIGHTED EYE

Eyeglasses to correct nearsightedness have negative lenses.

distant
object

lens

eyes may be corrected by wearing spectacles with positive (converging) lenses. An object now held at the normal
near point is seen or read distinctly. With age, the lens
of the eye loses some flexibility and the muscles attached to it lose some tone. This loss of accommodation varies among people. It can be corrected by glasses,
usually ground so the upper part of the lens gives a
correction for distant vision. The lower segment of these
bifocal glasses is a slightly thicker, positive lens for
close work or reading.

A nearsighted person can see objects clearly at close
range, but cannot focus on those at a distance. This
difficulty is remedied by glasses with negative (diverging)
lenses. With them, distant objects are seen as though
they were within his range of accommodation.

CONTACT LENSES are a form
of eyeglasses that fit directly
over the cornea of the eye, float-
ing on the layer of tears that
covers its surface. Such small
lenses correct severe refractive
eye conditions and have special
advantages for athletes, actors,
and others.

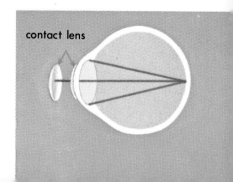

contact lens

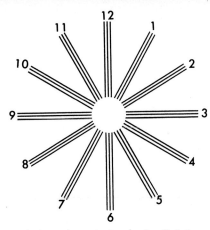

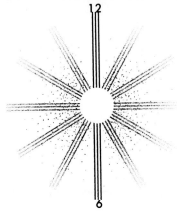

Astigmatism test chart. Rotate page at arm's length. All lines should appear equally intense.

For some persons with severe astigmatism, the test chart might look like this.

ASTIGMATISM of the eye is due to a fault in the curvature of the cornea or lens (page 85). If either curved surface is not symmetrical, rays in different planes will not be focused at the same distance behind the lens. Thus part of the image will be out of focus. This defect can usually be corrected by wearing spectacles with cylindrical lenses (below) instead of spherical ones. For large corrections or irregular corneas, contact lenses may be prescribed. Almost two out of three persons have at least a mild form of astigmatism.

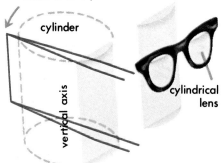

focus in one plane

cylinder

vertical axis

cylindrical lens

ASTIGMATIC GLASSES have cylindrical lenses, which are curved about a transverse axis rather than around a point, as in simple positive lenses. Cylindrical lenses can aid in correcting astigmatism, in which the lens of the eye does not have sufficient curvature around its vertical axis.

COMPOUND LENSES are used in precision optical instruments such as microscopes, telescopes, and expensive cameras. They consist of two or more simple lenses (elements) combined in such a way that the aberrations are minimized. The elements are sometimes cemented together and sometimes carefully spaced apart in the same mount. Desirable characteristics of an optical image are brightness, high resolution of fine detail, edge sharpness of the image, flatness of field, and good contrast between light and dark portions. All of these cannot be achieved at the same time, and even the best lens is a compromise, achieving one good quality partly at the expense of another. Computers are now used in lens design to help choose the proper curvatures, materials, and spacings of the elements for best correction of the aberrations.

Some image-forming instruments use both mirrors and lenses. Such systems, containing both refracting and reflecting elements, are called catadioptric.

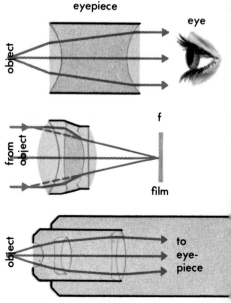

MAGNIFYING EYEPIECE is used in simple viewing and measuring instruments. One form is the pocket doublet magnifier. Careful lens grinding and spacing reduces aberrations.

TELEPHOTO LENS for a camera is a compound lens which gives the effect of a long focal length system with a relatively short lens-to-film distance.

MICROSCOPE OBJECTIVE LENS has a short focal length and relatively large aperture. Its high magnification emphasizes aberrations, so that a high order of correction is required.

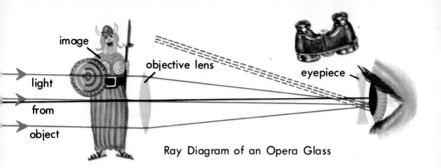

Ray Diagram of an Opera Glass

THE TELESCOPE was invented by a Dutch optician, Hans Lippershey, in 1608, some 300 years after the invention of spectacles. Galileo received news of this invention in 1609, and without seeing the original, he constructed a telescope consisting of one positive and one negative lens mounted in a discarded organ pipe. The same optical arrangement is used more efficiently in opera glasses, which are usually binocular. The positive lens is called the objective, and the negative lens is the ocular, or eyepiece. The field of view afforded by opera glasses is rather small at large magnifications, so opera glasses are usually of low power—3 to 5 magnifications. Since the eyepiece is a negative lens, the image seen by the viewer is upright.

The spyglass, or terrestrial telescope, provides an upright image because a third lens lies between the objective and ocular (below). This makes the instrument quite long; so, for convenience, it is usually made collapsible.

Ray diagram shows how inverted image is erected in a simple spyglass.

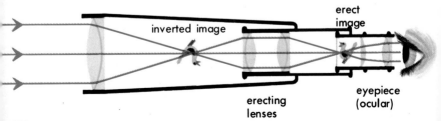

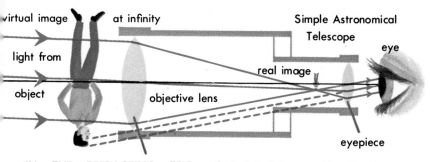

virtual image at infinity

Simple Astronomical Telescope

light from

eye

real image

object

objective lens

eyepiece

IN THE REFRACTING TELE-SCOPE the objective forms a real, inverted image of a distant object at the prime focus. The eyepiece then forms a magnified virtual image. Magnification depends on the ability of the objective to furnish enough light and a good image for high magnification by the eyepiece.

REFRACTING TELESCOPES use positive lenses for both objective and eyepiece. The real inverted image produced by the objective is viewed, enlarged, through the eyepiece. Refracting telescopes are limited to a maximum aperture of about one meter because of the difficulty of producing very large pieces of flawless optical-quality glass, and then grinding coaxial curvatures on both sides of the lens. Also, as lenses are made larger, the amount of light absorbed by the glass increases, and the weight of the lens causes it to sag, introducing optical errors. This type of telescope is used to study celestial bodies.

The refracting telescope at Yerkes Observatory in Wisconsin has an objective lens 40 inches in diameter, the largest used successfully by astronomers. The telescope has a theoretical magnifying power of 4,000 diameters.

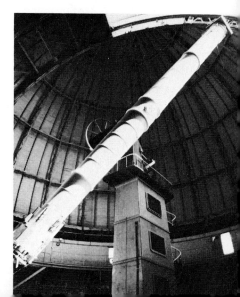

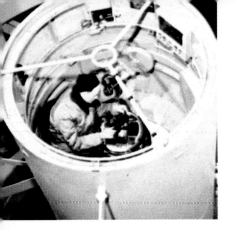

The Hale telescope on Palomar Mountain in Southern California has the largest mirror of any optical telescope. The disk of pyrex glass has a diameter of 200 in. and is 27 in. thick. It weighs 15 tons. The concave surface is coated with aluminum oxide. View here is of the "cage" in which the astronomer makes his observations.

REFLECTING TELESCOPES use curved mirrors instead of an objective lens. All telescopes over 40 inches in diameter are of the reflecting type. Since only the surface of a large mirror needs to be optically perfect, it can be braced from the back to prevent distortion. A waffle pattern molded into the back reduces the weight and maintains rigidity. The front surface of the mirror is carefully ground and polished to a paraboloid. It is then coated with a very thin aluminum film, which oxidizes into a highly reflecting and durable surface.

A 200-inch reflector collects four times as much light as a 100-inch instrument. It sees twice as far into space, and thus surveys a universe eight times as large as that seen by the smaller telescope.

In the reflecting telescope, light from astronomical objects is reflected from a curved mirror to a prime focus where an inverted real image is formed. In the Newtonian form, shown below, a flat mirror is placed in the beam to reflect the prime focus toward an eyepiece at the side of the instrument.

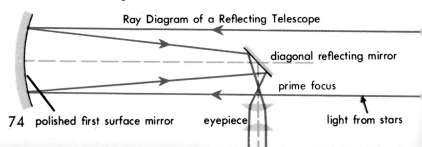

Ray Diagram of a Reflecting Telescope

diagonal reflecting mirror

prime focus

74   polished first surface mirror   eyepiece   light from stars

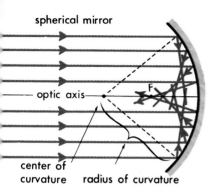

spherical mirror

optic axis

center of
curvature   radius of curvature

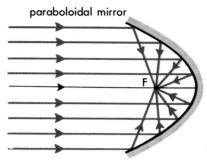

paraboloidal mirror

Light rays striking a spherical mirror parallel to the optic axis are not all reflected through the focal point (F). But in a parabo-loidal mirror, the changing curvature reflects all rays through the focal point, and a clear, sharp image results.

SPHERICAL ABERRATION OF CONCAVE MIRRORS is

similar to that of spherical lenses (p. 67). Parallel light rays that strike the mirror at different distances from the center are not reflected through the focal point. Since they do not meet at a single point, the resulting image is fuzzy. The defect becomes more serious as the diameter of the mirror is made larger in proportion to the radius of curvature.

To avoid spherical aberration, mirrors are made with concave paraboloidal surfaces. These are used in telescopes and searchlights.

SCHMIDT CAMERA is a form of telescope used to take pictures of large areas of the sky. Its field of view is wider than other reflectors because of a "correcting" lens inside. Since the field of focus is curved, this instrument cannot be used for "eye" observing. Shown is the 72-inch Schmidt Camera at Mount Palomar.

BINOCULARS are used, like a small telescope, to view distant objects. They employ an optical system of lenses and prisms to produce an enlarged erect image. The ocular and the objective lenses provide the magnification and illumination. Between them is a pair of 45–90–45 degree prisms (p. 60) so arranged that the light passing through the binoculars is internally reflected four times, making the image erect.

THREE FACTORS are involved in the usefulness of binoculars—magnification, field of view, and light-gathering power. Magnification must be suited to the purpose. Any movement by either the observer or the observed is magnified at high power. For hand-held uses, binoculars with magnifications of 6x to 8x are best. Higher magnifications require a tripod or other support. Field of view is largely determined by the ocular lenses. The diameter of the objective lens determines the light-gathering power—the larger the better if binoculars are used at night or in shady woods. Binoculars have central or individual focus (central preferred). They range in magnification from about 2 to 20. Each binocular has an identification mark such as 8 × 30 or 7 × 50. The first number is the magnification, the second the objective diameter in millimeters. An 8 × 30 glass has slightly greater magnification but distinctly less light-gathering power than a 7 × 50.

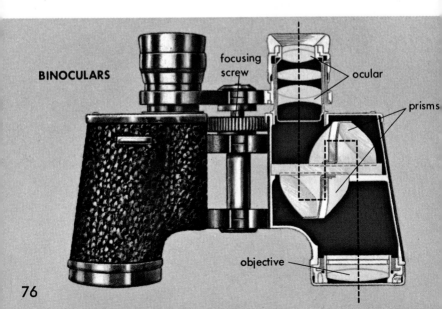

BINOCULARS

focusing screw

ocular

prisms

objective

MICROSCOPES, PROJECTORS AND ENLARGERS are similar in principle, but they differ in purpose and design. In each, a positive lens forms a real image of a brightly illuminated object. With projectors, the image is caught on a screen; with microscopes, it is viewed through an eyepiece; and with photographic enlargers, the image is projected on light sensitive paper, where it is recorded in semi-permanent form.

MICROSCOPES need intense illumination of the object because the image is much larger than the object and the same amount of light must be spread over a large area. The illumination is provided either by a tungsten lamp bulb or by an arc lamp, its light concentrated on the object by a lens or by a concave mirror used as a condenser. The microscope's objective lens has a short focal length (from 1 cm to less than 1 mm) and produces a sharp image of a very small field.

IMAGE SHARPNESS depends on resolving power rather than on magnifying power, and is limited by diffraction effects that blur the image. Two points separated by a distance less than one half the wavelength of light cannot be resolved optically and will appear as one point instead of two. With the usual illumination, this separation is approximately 1/100,000 of an inch.

THE ELECTRON MICROSCOPE, by using a beam of electrons with an effective wavelength much shorter than that of light, obtains over 100 times the resolving power of optical microscopes.

THE MAGNIFICATION achieved with an optical microscope is approximately equal to the power of the objective multiplied by the power of the ocular or eyepiece, producing an overall magnification of up to about 1,500 diameters.

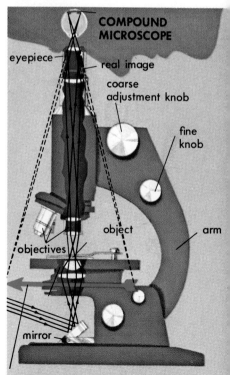

COMPOUND MICROSCOPE

eyepiece

real image

coarse adjustment knob

fine knob

object

arm

objectives

mirror

virtual image

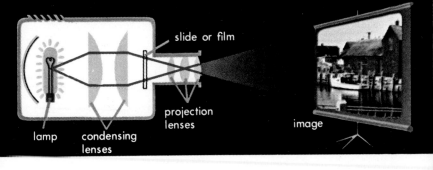

slide or film

projection lenses

image

lamp   condensing lenses

PROJECTORS use high-intensity tungsten or arc lamps for illumination. Two condensing lenses concentrate the light rays through the object (usually a film slide). The converging rays pass on through the projection lenses, and the enlarged image is thrown on a screen. This is an inverted image, so slides are inserted upside down in a projector. With any given combination of lenses, the farther the image is projected the larger it will be, and greater lamp intensity will be required. With some projectors (below), an opaque object can be reflected on the screen.

PHOTOGRAPHIC ENLARGERS are precision projectors with adjustments for focusing the image and controlling image size and brightness. Good enlargers provide uniform illumination, a good lens system, and a rigid mount. In operation, light from a lamp is concentrated by a paraboloidal reflector, passes through a diffusing glass (or a condensing lens), continues through the negative and then through the projection lens, which forms an enlarged image of the negative on the easel. Image sharpness is adjusted by moving the projection lens relative to the negative.

OPAQUE PROJECTOR

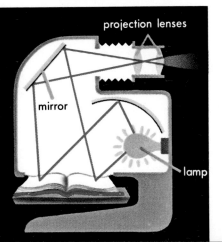

projection lenses

mirror

lamp

ENLARGER

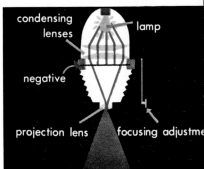

condensing lenses   lamp

negative

projection lens   focusing adjustme

easel

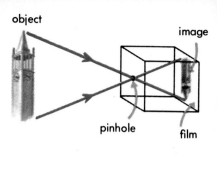

object

image

pinhole

film

Path of light in a pinhole camera

A pinhole camera photograph

CAMERA comes from the Latin phrase *camera obscura*, or dark chamber, for all picture-taking instruments have a dark chamber to protect the sensitive film from light. The simplest camera is a light-proof box with a pinhole in one end and a piece of film on the opposite inside wall. Light reaches the film only when the pinhole is uncovered, usually for a few seconds.

Use of a lens instead of a pinhole allows much more light to pass through, and the same picture can be taken in much shorter time. If the area of the lens is 1,000 times as large as the pinhole, the picture which required ten seconds can be made in 1/100 second, an average speed in many modern cameras.

In addition to a lens and film, a camera usually has a shutter, an adjustable diaphragm, and some type of focusing adjustment. The shutter prevents light from striking the film except when a picture is being made. A mechanism opens the shutter and closes it automatically after a length of time. Camera shutters may have speeds from 10 seconds to 1/1,000 of a second. Some cameras take pictures at a millionth of a second, enabling man to see the unseeable. The diaphragm can be adjusted to admit varying amounts of light each time the shutter is open. The focusing mechanism moves the lens back and forth to achieve a clear image.

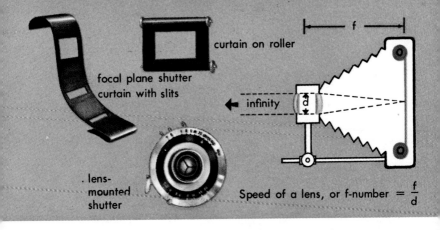

focal plane shutter curtain with slits

curtain on roller

← infinity

lens-mounted shutter

Speed of a lens, or f-number = $\dfrac{f}{d}$

THE SHUTTER of a camera allows light from the subject to enter the camera and strike the film for a time. Shutters are located either at the lens or at the film. Lens shutters are usually placed between or just behind the elements of the lens and usually have a set of leaves that snap open for the desired time and then snap shut. Focal plane shutters are next to the film and resemble a window blind with slots cut in it. A modern version has two curtains. As one moves and uncovers the film, the second follows so closely that the opening between them is a mere slot. Exposure time is varied by adjusting the width of the slot.

THE f-NUMBER of a lens refers to the ratio of its diameter (d) to its focal length (f). For example, f/8 refers to an aperture whose diameter is 1/8 of the focal length. A camera's lowest f-number corresponds to its wide-open diaphragm and is called the speed of the lens. Using a lower f-number shortens the required exposure time, but reduces the depth of field (p. 81). The diaphragm is set to the highest f-number that can be used with a given shutter speed in order to get maximum depth of field. Many modern cameras have a built-in photoelectric cell that selects automatically the lens opening for the shutter speed used.

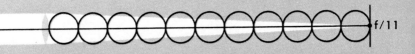

f/2

f/3.5

The relation of the diameter of a lens to its focal length is the f-number. For example, f/3.5 means the focal length of the lens is 3.5 times its diameter.

f/11

FOCUS is achieved when light from an object passes through a camera lens and forms a clear, accurate image on the film or viewer. Light rays from an object point diverge slightly as they enter a camera. With a wide-open lens, the rays pass through all parts of the lens and converge to the image point (below). To focus the camera, the distance from the lens to the film is adjusted so that the point of convergence will lie at the film surface—not before or behind it. It is impossible to focus all points of a three-dimensional scene on the film at the same time, but a satisfactory sharpness can usually be achieved over a considerable depth of the scene.

Adjustment is most critical when focusing on a nearby object with a wide-open lens. It is least critical for a distant object with the smallest lens opening. The accuracy of the focusing may be judged by observing the sharpness of the image on a translucent glass surface in reflex-type cameras or by superimposing two images in a rangefinder in some other cameras.

DEPTH OF FIELD is the depth of a scene that is in focus on the camera's film. A large lens aperture allows only a limited depth to be in focus. The rest of the scene is fuzzy. With a smaller opening, the cone of light rays from lens to film converges and diverges less. Both near and distant objects are in better focus.

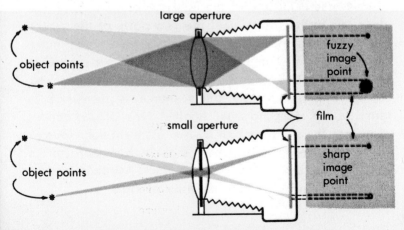

large aperture

object points

fuzzy image point

film

small aperture

object points

sharp image point

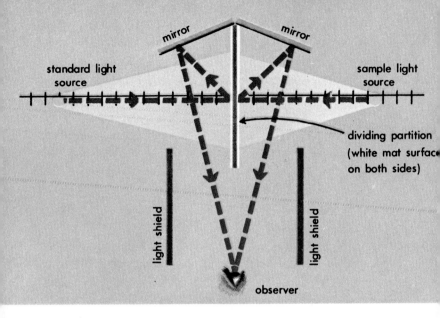

In this simple photometer, identical white surfaces are illuminated by the two different light sources being compared.

PHOTOMETERS are instruments for comparing the intensities of two light sources which have approximately the same hue. The two sources are arranged so that they illuminate adjacent parts of the same visual field, usually a screen. One of the light sources is then moved closer or farther away until the two parts of the screen match in brightness. The average observer can make such a match with an error of less than two per cent. One light source is usually a standard lamp of known intensity, so the intensity of the other source is measured in terms of the standard one. Another type of photometer compares the shadows cast by two adjacent light sources and gives similar information. Light-bulb manufacturers use photometers to test their product. Astronomers use them to measure the light intensity of stars.

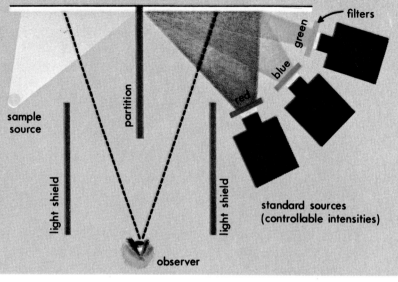

Both sides of the divided screen are viewed simultaneously in this colorimeter to determine the sample's color characteristics.

COLORIMETERS are instruments designed to measure color characteristics other than intensity. In one type, one part of a divided field is illuminated by light from the source being studied; the other part by a mixture of light from three standard sources, each of a different hue (p. 101). By adjusting the amounts of light from the standard sources, the operator can match the two parts of the field so that they look exactly alike. Sometimes one of the standard sources must be used on the same part of the field with the test source, achieving the match with the other two standard sources. No more than three standard sources are ever required.

Simple color matching with indicator chemicals is a part of chemical analysis. This type of colorimeter is more properly called a color comparator.

SEEING LIGHT AND COLOR

The eye is often compared to a camera. It has a lens that produces an inverted image on the retina, whose surface is sensitive to light just as film is. In front, the eye has an iris that changes the size of the pupil, performing the same function as the diaphragm of a camera. The pupil is simply the hole in the iris through which light enters the eye. As its size changes, the pupil admits more or less light as needed, depending on the amount of illumination present. This adaptation by the iris to the level of illumination is continued by the retina (p. 86).

A ray of light entering the eye passes through the transparent cornea, the aqueous humor, the lens, and the vitreous humor. All help focus the light before it strikes the rods and cones, which are photoreceptors located on the retina. Here is where the actual process of seeing begins. The greatest bending of light rays occurs at the first surface of the cornea.

A group of ligaments and muscles automatically control the shape of the lens to bring objects at different distances into focus on the retina. This process is called accommodation (p. 68). As one gets older, the lens gradually loses its flexibility, and the ability to accommodate decreases.

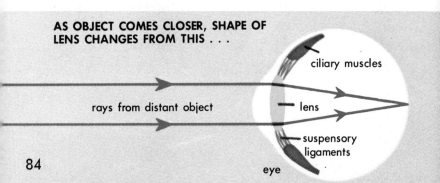

AS OBJECT COMES CLOSER, SHAPE OF LENS CHANGES FROM THIS . . .

ciliary muscles

rays from distant object

lens

suspensory ligaments

eye

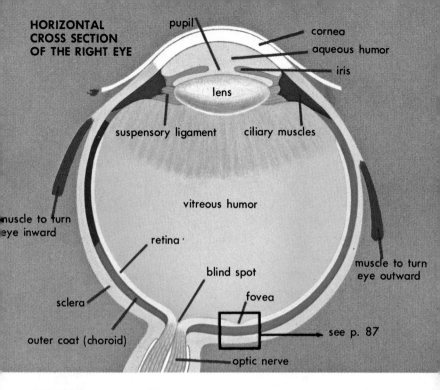

HORIZONTAL CROSS SECTION OF THE RIGHT EYE

pupil

cornea

aqueous humor

iris

lens

suspensory ligament

ciliary muscles

muscle to turn eye inward

vitreous humor

retina

blind spot

fovea

muscle to turn eye outward

sclera

outer coat (choroid)

see p. 87

optic nerve

THE LENS is supported by a suspensory ligament that holds it in tension within the encircling ciliary muscles. When relaxed, the ciliary muscle holds the ligament taut, and the lens is flattened for viewing distant objects. When focusing on nearby objects the muscle contracts, loosening the suspensory ligament to let the lens assume its natural bulging shape. Thus the lens is thin for viewing distant objects (p. 84, bottom) and becomes thicker to focus on near ones (below). It is impossible to have near and distant objects in sharp focus at the same time.

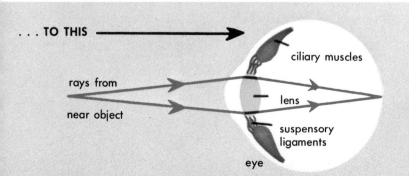

. . . TO THIS

ciliary muscles

rays from

near object

lens

suspensory ligaments

eye

85

THE RETINA is the eye's sensitive inner surface. It is a complex system of nerve endings formed of two kinds of light-sensitive cells: rods and cones, named for the shapes of their tips. The rods are most numerous and predominate near the edges of the retina. Cones are interspersed with the rods, but near the center of the retina is an area consisting almost entirely of cones. This is the yellow spot (macula lutea) with a small depression (fovea centralis) in its middle. Distinct vision occurs only for the part of the image that falls on the fovea, and since this covers an angle only slightly larger than one degree, an object may be "seen" in detail only by scanning it. At the fovea, each cone is connected to its own optic nerve fiber. Elsewhere in the retina, which contains some 115 million rods and 7 million cones, about 80 receptors are connected to a single nerve fiber.

Electrical impulses from the rod and cone cells travel along the optic nerve to the optic lobe of the brain, where the mental picture of the scene is registered.

COLOR VISION (cone cells) does not operate at very low levels of illumination. By moonlight, hues vanish, and only shades of gray remain. Unlike the cones, the rods can adapt to very dim light by increasing their sensitivity. They thus provide a coarse but useful vision even by starlight. Under such conditions you may detect an object out of the corner of your eye (rod vision) that cannot be seen when you look directly at it.

The rods sense only brightness. Cones sense both brightness and hue. Rod vision is much more sensitive to flicker and motion than is cone vision.

THE VISUAL IMPULSE is produced by the changing of visual purple (rhodopsin) to retinene. Rhodopsin undergoes chemical changes under the influence of light photons that result in bleaching of the rhodopsin to pale-yellow retinene. The strength of the brightness sensation depends on the rate of bleaching.

Since sensitivity of the rods depends on the amount of visual purple present, its regeneration must be fast and sufficient. This regeneration occurs most rapidly in the dark and is related to the amount of vitamin A present. Lack of vitamin A retards regeneration, causing night blindness.

LIGHT ENTERING THE EYE reaches the photochemical ends of the rods and cones only after passing through the network of nerve cells and ganglia that lies above them. These tip ends of the rods and cones are embedded in a layer of epithelium containing pigment granules that optically isolate the rods and cones. The ganglia above these layers sort visual impulses, and the nerve fibers transmit them to the brain.

STRUCTURE OF RETINA, head-on view (right) and sectional view (below), centered on the fovea.

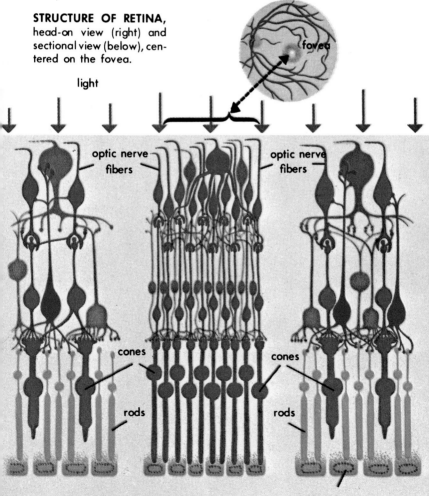

fovea

light

optic nerve fibers

optic nerve fibers

cones

cones

rods

rods

pigment layer

THE OPTIC NERVE is the most important nerve of the eye because it carries visual signals to the brain. Various motor nerves operate muscles controlling the movement of the eyeball and upper eyelid and the thickness of the lens. The optic nerve is a thick bundle of nerve fibers connected to the rear of the retina at a spot slightly off-center toward the nose. No rods or cones cover this spot so it is insensitive to light. To detect this blind spot close the left eye and stare at the black dot at the lower left corner of this page, holding the page about 18 inches from the nose. Move the page around till the dot in the lower right-hand corner (p. 89) becomes invisible. The left-hand dot will disappear if you look with the left eye only at the right-hand dot. No blind spot is apparent with both eyes open, because the fields of vision overlap.

The optic nerve from each eye leads to the visual area of the brain at the extreme back of the head. Injury to this area can cause blindness. In front of this region, in areas that are poorly defined, complex visual association takes place.

The optic nerve fibers from the right eye appear to lead to the left side of the brain; those from the left eye seem to go to the right side of the brain. Where they cross is the optic chiasma. Actually there is not a complete crossing that affects all the nerve fibers but an intermixing. Nerves from the right half of the retina of both eyes go to the right half of the brain and record the left half of the field of vision.

VISUAL FIELDS An object in the right half of the visual field registers on the left half of each retina and in the left side of the brain. In the diagram, colored ovals represent overlapping visual fields. The round, darker central area is the visual field of the fovea of the retina. Areas seen by a single eye (monocular fields) are shown in lighter colors.

THE OPTIC CHIASMA, where nerve fibers from the inner sides of the retina cross over to the opposite hemisphere of the brain, is just behind the eyes. Nerve fibers from the outer sides of the retina also pass through the optic chiasma, but remain on outer optic pathways.

THE VISUAL CENTERS of the brain are at the rear of the right and left lobes. In forming a mental picture, an object on an individual's right stimulates cells in the left lobe.

based on Ciba Collection of Medical Illustrations by F. Netter, M.D. © CIBA

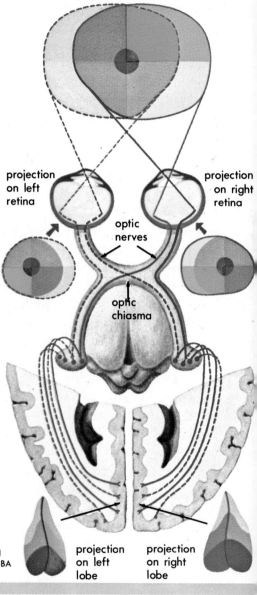

projection on left retina

projection on right retina

optic nerves

optic chiasma

projection on left lobe

projection on right lobe

THE HUMAN EYE is the most versatile of all radiation detectors. Within the retina of the eye a chemical response to radiation is translated into electrical pulses. These very weak electrical messages travel almost instantaneously to the brain along the optic nerve fibers. The sensation of sight occurs in the brain. Because of psychological factors, the quality of visual sensations cannot be translated into physical data and there is no way to compare the visual sensations of different people with accuracy. What you see is for the most part subjective—wholly within the mind, and therefore usually not measurable.

Within your brain, other bodily sensations—taste, touch, smell, and sound—are automatically correlated with the visual one. The brain compares the result with remembered sensations from past experience, modifies them according to your attitude and intent, and then produces in your conscious mind information about what you see. This information constitutes your perception or awareness of objects. Your perception may be correct or incorrect, depending in part upon attitudes and experience. An illusion is a faulty perception caused by some unusual presentation of the scene or by some prejudice or emotion of the observer. He may or may not be aware that the scene is not what it appears to be.

The sight of an object gives information about its size, shape, color, texture, location, and motion. Just how these features can be determined from the light emitted or reflected from an object and its surroundings is a major problem in psychology. The physical processes of seeing are fairly well understood, and current research is providing answers to the physiology of vision. Much remains to be learned about the psychological aspects of an individual's perception.

DISTANCE, DEPTH AND MOTION are affected by several kinds of cues which are noted automatically and often unconsciously. You use such cues as convergence, superposition, elevation, brightness, distinctness, and known size to place objects mentally near or far in a scene. These same cues lend a partial feeling of reality to ordinary two-dimensional pictures and are effective even when one eye is closed.

CONVERGENCE of lines is frequently a useful cue in the judging of distances. Distant objects form smaller images on the retina of the eye than do nearby objects. The problem is to determine whether a particular object is small and close by, or large and far away. In a picture, the convergence of lines may indicate recession from a viewer. Parallel lines of a highway seem to meet at the horizon. Every artist knows he must draw them this way to make them look real. The art of making a three-dimensional scene appear real on a two-dimensional surface is called perspective.

left
vanishing
point

right
vanishing
point

Lines often converge in two directions in perspective drawings.

SUPERPOSITION, known also as overlay, is a powerful depth cue. When one object overlaps another and partially obscures it, then the first object appears to be nearer. In the illustration above, the jack seems closer to the camera. The actual arrangement is shown at the right. Simply changing the angle of view discloses the true position, with the clipped queen actually closer to the camera than the jack.

ELEVATION is another depth cue. In a picture of a landscape, the horizon is always higher than the foreground. Objects that are higher or farther from the bottom of the picture always appear to be a greater distance away. In the pictures below, elevation makes the tree at the right seem farther away and larger than the tree to the left. The building appears larger in the picture to the left, but both trees and buildings are the same size.

BRIGHTNESS DIFFERENCES may give a false depth cue. This can be demonstrated easily, as in the illustration here. When other distance cues are carefully concealed, the apparent relative distance of two playing cards depends on their illumination. The card that is given more illumination and seems brighter than the other appears to be the nearer. Both cards, however, are actually the same distance from the viewer.

DISTINCTNESS—or sharp edges and clear details—also implies closeness. Haze and fog enhance the appearance of depth. They make distant objects less distinct than those nearby, and some not-so-distant objects become blurred. This tends to compress the scale of distances. Sometimes in a fog nearby objects appear unnaturally large (right) because the viewer unconsciously compares them to what he believes are more distant objects.

Distinctness is affected also by a factor inherent in the lens of the eye and also in the lenses of cameras. When the lens is focused on a particular object, anything nearer or farther away will be slightly out of focus. This effect is minimized in a photograph taken with a very small lens opening (p. 81). Objects of equal distinctness are then judged to be equally distant, if other cues are absent. The loss of perspective in such cases is shown here in the photograph making it appear that the pole is growing out of the girl's head.

KNOWN (OR IMAGINED) SIZE of objects is probably the most important cue to distance. When a card is placed in a spotlight in a darkened room, a viewer estimates its distance based on his prior knowledge of the card's size. If a larger card is then substituted, he changes his estimate in direct proportion to the change in the card's size. Photographs that exaggerate the size of fish employ the association of depth perception with size determination. In the above illustration, the size of the hand and of the man are cues to the size of the fish. First cover the hand and then the man. The fish will first appear larger, then smaller.

MOTION PARALLAX accounts for the apparent motion of objects seen from a moving car. If you stare at one object some distance from the side of the road, the trees beyond it seem to be moving forward in the same direction as the car, but telephone poles near the road move back the other way. The whole scene appears to rotate about the object on which you fix your gaze. This is shown below. The person is moving from A to B. The post appears to move backward, the tree forward. The same effect is obtained by turning your head. It is an important factor in the visual perception of distance.

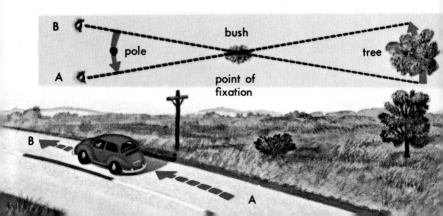

BINOCULAR CUES to depth perception require the cooperation of both eyes. All the cues mentioned so far are monocular cues—that is, they can be seen with either eye alone.

BINOCULAR VISION produces a kind of stationary parallax—a very slight difference in the appearance and apparent location of objects because your eyes view objects from slightly different positions. For objects nearer than about 100 feet, the images formed in the left and right eyes are, in fact, slightly different views. The mind interprets this difference in terms of depth, enhancing your perception of a real, three-dimensional scene instead of a flat, two-dimensional picture. Binocular parallax is the major factor in the space perception of nearby objects. This effect is totally lacking in ordinary pictures, but occurs in the images that you see in mirrors. For very close objects the muscular effort of converging your

eyes on the point of focus gives you another indication of the distances of objects.

A stereo camera illustrates binocular vision. It has two lenses separated by the same distance as between the eyes, about 2½ inches. The two pictures obtained with a stereo camera are slightly different and correspond to the views seen by the right and left eyes. If the pictures are arranged so that the left eye sees only the picture taken by the left lens and the right eye only the picture taken by the right lens, the appearance of depth is produced. To get a stereo view of the pictures shown below, hold a piece of paper or cardboard between your eyes so that you view the left and right pictures with the corresponding eye.

These two pictures were made with a stereo camera.

ILLUSIONS occur when our perception is distorted by an unusual or deceptive presentation of an object or by some prejudice or emotion about it. Our faith in the usual accuracy of our visual perceptions is strong enough to support the adage: "Seeing is believing." But we are often fooled by our eyes. What we see is strongly influenced by what we think we see or by what we want to see.

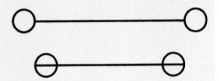

The two lines are of equal length but placing the circles farther out makes the upper line appear longer.

An elliptical frame may appear circular because shading and perspective lead you to expect it to be circular.

In distorted Ames' room (below) the left corner of the room is much farther away than the right.

Both men are about the same height. A floor plan reveals in part how illusion was created.

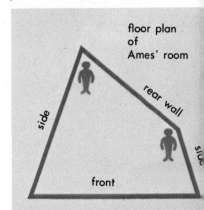

floor plan
of
Ames' room

rear wall

side

side

front

Concentric circles appear to make a spiral (right). Even when the observer is informed that this is an illusion, he is unable to see it otherwise. A draftsman's compass can be used to prove that all arcs have a common center.

The two horizontal lines (below) are parallel, but the arrangement of the other lines makes the horizontal lines seem to pull apart at the center.

Indentations appear as depressions (left below) and as raised surfaces (right below) because the observer interprets the light as coming from above. The photos are identical; one is inverted.

Raindrops change sunlight into a primary rainbow by refraction and by a single reflection of the rays within each drop. This action makes visible the colors already present in the light.

Inside the water droplets of a secondary bow, the light rays are reflected twice, reversing the order of the spectrum. A viewer sees each color at a different angle relative to the sun.

THE NATURE OF COLOR

In 1630 the French philosopher Descartes attributed the color of an object to a change in the light when it is reflected from the object. Until that time it had been thought that light had no color; that color belonged to objects and that light merely made it visible. The modern concept of color follows Descartes' point of view. Color, like light, is a psychophysical concept, depending upon both radiant energy (the physical stimulus) and visual sensations (the psychological response). Color and light are closely related terms. By definition, color includes all aspects of light except variations in time and space. For example, the distribution of sunlight and shadows on a lawn is not concerned with the color of the light. Nor does the flickering of a candle flame change the color of the light.

COLOR is one aspect of your visual experience when you look at an object. The color you see depends on the intensity and wavelengths of the light that illuminates the object, on the wavelengths of light reflected or transmitted by the object, on the color of the surrounding objects, and on absorption or reflection by substances in the light path.

In a space capsule, the sky appears black. From the ground, it looks blue because of scattering by atmospheric particles. A cloud may be white where the sunlight illuminates it from above or gray where sunlight does not strike directly, or it may possess any of the hues of a tropical sunset. The cloud does not change color, but our perception of its color changes.

THE COLOR OF WATER varies. An observer flying over the Florida Keys might well see the adjacent ocean areas as green, blue-green, and blue. A photograph, such as the one shown at right, can capture this same effect. Shallow, clear water with a sandy bottom will produce a light green because of the combination of the yellow reflected from the bottom and the reflection of the blue sky. As the water gets deeper, it becomes blue-green because there is more scattered blue light from the sky and less yellow reflected from the bottom. When the water is very deep with no reflection from the bottom, the water is a deep blue, particularly noticeable in the Gulf Stream. At no time is the color a property of the water. It is due to many causes and is best described as a characteristic of the light received by your eye.

THE PSYCHOLOGICAL ASPECTS of color sensation are hue, saturation and brightness. None of these is directly measurable. Since measurable physical aspects do not accurately specify color, the answers must be found in a combination of the two—the psychophysical variables: dominant wavelength, purity, and luminance.

The eye cannot distinguish the component wavelengths in a color sample. Two lights of different colors when mixed produce a third color, and no human eye can detect its composite nature. Scientists working with color try to predict the results of such color mixtures. They aim to describe and measure colors as accurately as possible. This can be done for the physical part of color. The energy distribution of the light can be plotted as shown below. But the color sensation of the observer— his response to the light entering his eyes—cannot be shown in the same way.

ENERGY at various wavelengths is shown on the two graphs below. A vertical solid line on each represents the same green color (in rectangle), which is tinted with white light. In the left graph, the white is that of daylight, a light mixture of many wavelengths. In the right graph, the white is a combination of monochromatic yellow and monochromatic blue. The brain interprets this mixture as white. If the intensities of the daylight and the yellow and blue light are adjusted with the green of the solid line to give the same tint, the eye sees the same tint of green in both cases, even though the spectral compositions are quite different.

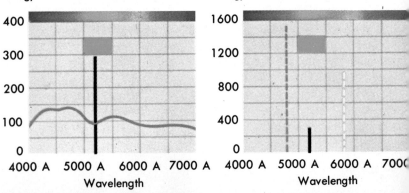

Energy

| 400 | 300 | 200 | 100 | 0 |

4000 A   5000 A   6000 A   7000 A
Wavelength

Energy

| 1600 | 1200 | 800 | 400 | 0 |

4000 A   5000 A   6000 A   7000 A
Wavelength

HUE	SATURATION	BRIGHTNESS
blue	pale magenta	white
green		gray
yellow		grayer
red	dark magenta	

The three types of color sensations

HUE is the color sensation by which you distinguish the different parts of the spectrum—red, blue, green, yellow, etc. The psychophysical variable related to hue is the dominant wavelength of the light for each color. Most light samples can be color-matched by adding the proper spectrally pure (monochromatic) light to white light. For these light samples there is only one spectrally pure light that will give a perfect match. The wavelength of that light is called the dominant wavelength of the sample and is a measurable quantity.

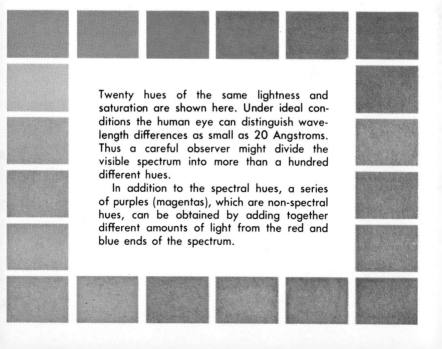

Twenty hues of the same lightness and saturation are shown here. Under ideal conditions the human eye can distinguish wavelength differences as small as 20 Angstroms. Thus a careful observer might divide the visible spectrum into more than a hundred different hues.

In addition to the spectral hues, a series of purples (magentas), which are non-spectral hues, can be obtained by adding together different amounts of light from the red and blue ends of the spectrum.

Saturation of red from low at the left to high at the right.

SATURATION refers to the degree of hue in a color. It is the color sensation by which you distinguish a hue as being pale or rich, weak or strong. Pink, for example, usually denotes a red of low saturation, while scarlet is a highly saturated red.

PURITY is the psychophysical quality most closely related to saturation. The purity of a color sample is the ratio of the amount of monochromatic light to the amount of white light in a mixture required to match the sample. Monochromatic light has 100 per cent purity; white light has zero.

Colors of the same purity do not all have the same saturation. The two are closely related but not identical. Pure yellow, for example, is much less saturated than pure violet. Luminance (p. 32) also affects saturation. Blues, reds, and purples appear more saturated at low luminance. Yellows and cyans (blue-greens) need higher luminance to achieve the same degree of saturation. After a certain point an increase in luminance decreases saturation.

The two reds below are of the same dominant wavelength but of different purity and will appear to be of the same hue but of different saturation.

HIGH PURITY

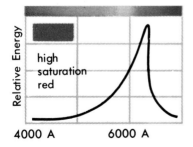

Relative Energy

high saturation red

4000 A   6000 A

Wavelength

LOW PURITY

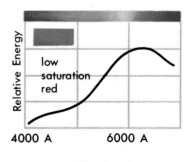

Relative Energy

low saturation red

4000 A   6000 A

Wavelength

SCALES of saturation and hue are combined here in a single diagram. The color blocks in the circular scale show how one hue blends into another. Each hue has the same lightness (p. 35) and satura- tion. Color blocks in the spokes show gradations in saturation from zero at the center to a maximum at the outer block. Other spokes could be added, one spoke for each hue in the circular scale.

BRIGHTNESS (p. 32) is the primary visual sensation by which you detect the presence of light. It is associated with the quantity of the light and the intensity of the visual sensation. Luminance, easily measured, is the psychophysical variable usually associated with brightness.

Although hue, saturation, and brightness may be separately identified as color sensation variables, they are not independent of one another. When one variable is changed the other two are often affected. Decreasing the brightness, for example, can cause a change in the saturation or even in the hue of the color.

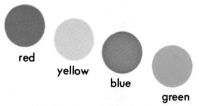

red
yellow
blue
green

PSYCHOLOGIST'S PRIMARIES

red
yellow
blue

ARTIST'S PRIMARIES

PRIMARY COLORS are simply hues you start with to mix others. Designating certain hues as primaries is an arbitrary convention that depends on who makes the selection and whether lights or object colors are used.

Blue, green, and red are usually used as the physicist's primaries in light experiments. However, any three widely separated monochromatic colors can serve. The psychological primaries are blue, green, red, and yellow, for each seems to invoke a singular response which does not involve any of the other colors. All other colors may be described in terms of these. The same color term used by different groups of people may, however, refer to markedly dissimilar colors.

Red, yellow, and blue are the artist's primaries. By mixing appropriate amounts of these pigments, almost any other hue can be produced. The artist is dealing with object colors; the physicist is working with colored lights; the psychologist is interested in both.

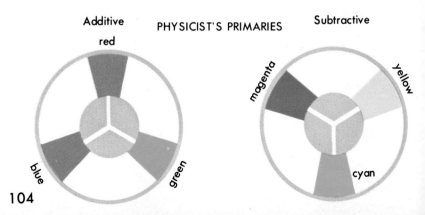

Additive   PHYSICIST'S PRIMARIES   Subtractive
red

blue   green

magenta   yellow

cyan

COMPLEMENTARY HUES are any two hues which produce white when mixed together in some proportion. ("White" here refers to any hueless, or achromatic, light. At low luminance it would be called gray.) Every hue has a complementary hue. The two hues of a complementary pair are widely separated in the spectrum. The complement of red is blue-green; the complement of yellow is blue. Complementaries of the greens are purples, hues not found in the spectrum.

Mixing of complementary lights does not produce intermediate hues. With proper adjustment of the intensities of two complementary lights, white light is obtained. Thus white light can be produced by many combinations of complementary lights.

The curve shows complementary wavelengths for the standard observer. Perpendiculars extended to the two scales from any point on the curve will reveal the wavelengths of two complementary hues. Complementaries to green cannot be obtained from the graph.

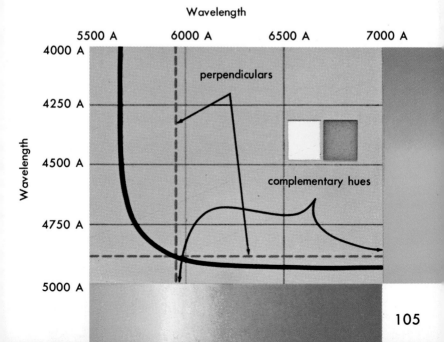

COLOR MIXTURES may be achieved by either additive or subtractive methods. The blending of colored lights from more than one source is additive, while the passage of light through successive colored absorbers (filters) is subtractive. Pigment mixing is mainly subtractive even though paints are added to one another. It is subtractive because pigments absorb (subtract) some wavelengths of the light striking them and reflect the remaining wavelengths which you see. Additive mixtures of red, green, and blue lights of proper relative luminance produce white where all overlap, and cyan, magenta, and yellow where they overlap in pairs (below).

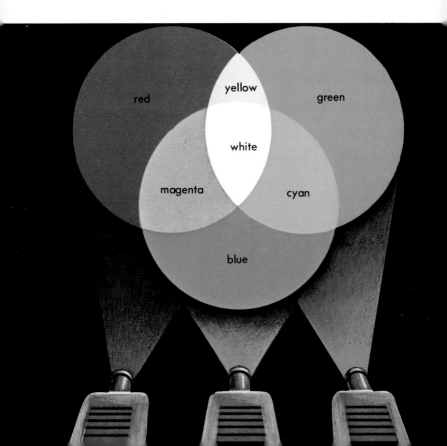

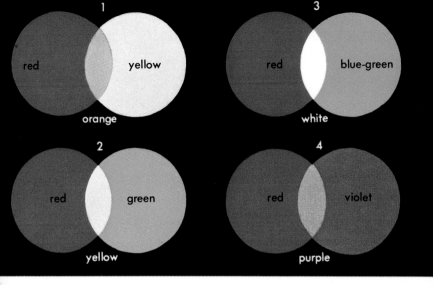

1	3
red / yellow — orange	red / blue-green — white

2	4
red / green — yellow	red / violet — purple

ADDITIVE COLOR MIXING is easily accomplished by projecting pure (monochromatic) lights from two or more projectors onto a white screen. Each projector is equipped with a set of filters which permit it to produce light of any desired wavelength. When a beam of red light is projected so that it overlaps a beam of yellow light (1, above), the result is orange. If the relative intensities of the two projectors are adjusted, it is possible to change gradually the hue of the mixture from orange toward either red or yellow. If the red light is kept constant and the yellow light made more green, the hue of the mixture becomes yellower (2), and the saturation becomes less and less. Finally, a wavelength in the blue-green will be reached at which the mixture will lose all hue, becoming achromatic, or white (3). Thus red and the blue-green are complementary hues. If the variable light is changed from blue-green to violet and the red still kept constant, a non-spectral purple (4) results.

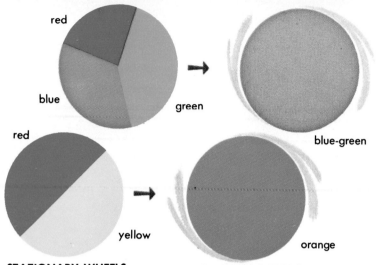

red **green** → **blue-green**

blue

red → **orange**

yellow

STATIONARY WHEELS   **SPINNING WHEELS**

OTHER ADDITIVE METHODS of mixing colors, in addition to using two or more colored beams from separate projectors (p. 107), include the placing of filters in rapid succession in front of a single projector. This makes use of the persistence of vision—the retention of an image for a fraction of a second after the stimulus has ceased. Images presented in rapid succession fuse into one another to form a composite image. A simple device using this effect is the color wheel. By adjusting the size of the colored sectors and spinning the wheel rapidly, different hues may be produced (above) including neutral gray (below). The hues are rather unsaturated and the luminance normally is not sufficient to make the gray seem "white."

STATIONARY WHEEL   **SPINNING WHEEL**

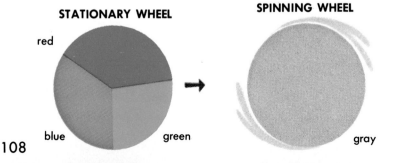

red → **gray**

blue   **green**

In the fall when the leaves have changed color, distant views of the landscape provide excellent examples of natural additive mixing. The colors of individual leaves fuse to give a single color to a tree, and farther away all the trees blend into a single hue.

MOSAIC FUSION is the term used to describe the way your eye mixes the colors of individual leaves in an autumn landscape, the dots of a color television screen, or the individual colors of sand grains on a distant beach. When there are three or four point sources of colored light widely separated, they are focused separately on the retina, and the eye sees them as distinct colors. This separate focusing is called resolving.

If the point sources are moved closer together, eventually they will all be focused within the same group of rods and cones on the retina. They cannot be resolved any longer, but are seen as a single area even though they are distinct point sources. The color sensed is a mixed color, its hue depending on the spectral qualities of the colors of which it is composed.

If you increase the resolving power of your eye by examining a small area of a page of colored comic strips under a hand lens, you will see that there are numerous dots of different hues. Without the lens, adjacent dots blend together and form a single hue.

SUBTRACTIVE COLOR MIXING occurs whenever light passes through two or more selectively absorbing materials. Dyes, and also pigments, may be mixed together to form a single coloring agent (colorant) that will produce selective absorption. Separate filters which are traversed by the light in any order also cause subtractive color mixing. Even surface films from which the light is successively reflected subtract light. The process is called "subtractive" because the films or filters subtract certain portions of the spectrum from the incident light, leaving the remainder with a hue complementary to that subtracted. A piece of glass which absorbs the blue and green wavelengths of white light appears red because it transmits only the longer wavelengths. If the glass absorbs the green, it transmits a mixture of red and blue—magenta.

At each wavelength, the filter obeys the law of absorption (p. 51). The filters not only change the color of the light, but they reduce its intensity. If additional filters of the same type and thickness are placed in the light path, each will absorb the same fraction of the light. That is, if one thickness transmits ½ of the light, two thicknesses will transmit ¼,

Examples of subtractive color mixing are shown below with paints (pigments) and filters. In the former the colors that are not absorbed are reflected from the surface. In filters the colors not absorbed are transmitted through the filter.

PIGMENTS   **FILTERS**

Blue +   Yellow =   Green

Crimson +   Yellow =   Orange

yellow

red   green

magenta   blue   cyan

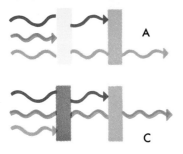
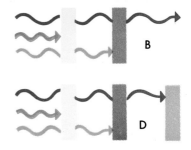
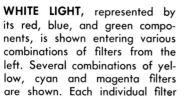

WHITE LIGHT, represented by its red, blue, and green components, is shown entering various combinations of filters from the left. Several combinations of yellow, cyan and magenta filters are shown. Each individual filter allows all but one of the colors entering it to pass. Each pair of filters (as in A, B, and C) allows a different part of the white light to pass through. In the last example (D), no light passes the third filter.

three thicknesses will transmit ⅛, and so on. When a filter consists of a colorant dissolved in a solvent, doubling the concentration of the colorant is equivalent to doubling the thickness.

The appearance of a colored filter may give little indication of its spectral absorption curve. Two filters that appear identical may transmit light of different colors when combined with another colored filter.

The artist who is familiar with his paints can more easily predict the results of his mixtures. He knows that mixing Thalo Blue, Alizarin Crimson, and white in the proper proportions will produce lavender. For him, subtractive color mixing is a matter of experience.

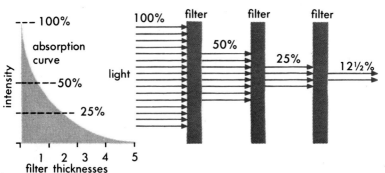

COLOR MATCHING is the physical process of adjusting a color mixture until it appears to be visually the same as a sample color. The manufacturers of paints and dyes, of textiles and plastics, of toys and cars, and of books and magazines, as well as those who print color film, are vitally concerned with good color matching.

Either additive mixing of colored lights or subtractive mixing using filters may be utilized to achieve a color match. Any color of the spectrum can be matched by the addition of monochromatic light to white light. Purple, a mixture of red and violet, is not a color of the spectrum and cannot be matched by this method because it lacks a single dominant wavelength. But a purple color can be identified by the wavelength of its complementary color. Light of this color mixed with purple light produces a colorless light.

Various color matching systems (p. 125) and colorimeters (p. 83) are available. Color standards—sets of color patches arranged systematically for visual comparison—are often preferred to colorimeters. Color standards and colorimeters can be calibrated in similar units and data can be converted from one system to the other.

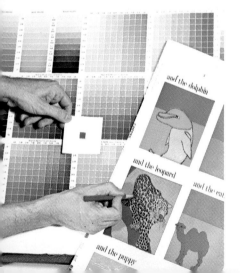

COLOR CHARTS are useful tools in the matching of colors. Printers use color charts that give in numbers or percentage the dot value of different inks that is required to reproduce a given color. The color squares that provide this information usually have punched holes so that the color in a square can be easily compared to the color in the illustration to be reproduced.

In old color vision tests, the testees sorted wool skeins by hue, trying to select all skeins that accurately matched the large one.

COLOR BLINDNESS is an everyday term referring to any pronounced deviation from normal color vision. The three major forms of color abnormality are anomalous trichromatism (a less severe departure from normal vision), dichromatism (partial color blindness), and monochromatism (complete color blindness).

The normal observer, known as a trichromat, can match any color with one, two, or three colored lights. Under controlled conditions, most trichromats will use about the same combination of selected lights to match any particular color. An individual who must arrive at his color match in a markedly different way from the average trichromat is said to have abnormal color vision. This is usually an inherited defect. It becomes evident in many school and home situations and is confirmed when the individual is asked to match two colors or to distinguish between different hues.

The cause of abnormal color vision is not fully known. There may be some defect in the cones of the retina, since it is the cones that distinguish color. There may be too much or too little of essential pigments in the eye. In rare cases, the optic nerve between the eye and the brain may not function properly.

About eight per cent of the male population and less than one per cent of females are born with defective color vision. Abnormal color vision can also be acquired.

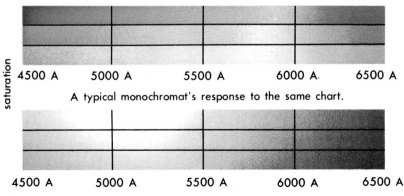

color to be matched

color matching by normal observer

color matching by anomalous trichromat

ANOMALOUS TRICHROMATISM is found in about three-fourths of all people with abnormal color vision. An anomalous trichromat sees colors, but not normally. He can match any color with a mixture of three colored lights, but will require different amounts of these lights than the normal observer. He is poor at mixing or matching colors. If his vision is green weak (the commonest type), he will need more than the normal amount of green in a green-red mixture to match a particular yellow. Other anomalous trichromats have red or blue weaknesses.

MONOCHROMATISM, or complete color blindness, is very rare. Only about one person in 30,000 is afflicted. In its typical inherited form, equally common in men and women, the monochromat depends solely on rod vision. Since his eye lacks the high resolution of the foveal cones, his visual acuity is low. The monochromat is unable to distinguish any colors. He can see only differences in brightness and can match all lights with a single light. Relative luminosity is his only criterion as shown in the comparison of normal and monochromatic spectra below.

Hue and saturation as viewed by a normal observer.

saturation

4500 A 5000 A 5500 A 6000 A 6500 A

A typical monochromat's response to the same chart.

4500 A 5000 A 5500 A 6000 A 6500 A

DICHROMATISM occurs in about 2 per cent of white males, but in only 0.03 per cent of females. About one-quarter of all people with defective color vision are dichromats. A dichromat can match all colors with mixtures of two primary lights rather than the three used by a normal observer.

One common form of dichromatism is red-green blindness which permits the individual to see only two colors—yellow and blue. A neutral gray is seen instead of blue-green and purple. Dark reds, greens, and grays are confused, and sensitivity to brightness is decreased by about half. In a similar, equally common condition, a person sees colors like the dichromat but gets no reaction at all from the long-wavelength end of the spectrum.

Still rarer are those kinds of defective color vision in which a person does not see yellow and blue. These conditions may involve lack of sensitivity to short waves.

HUE AND SATURATION COLOR WHEELS

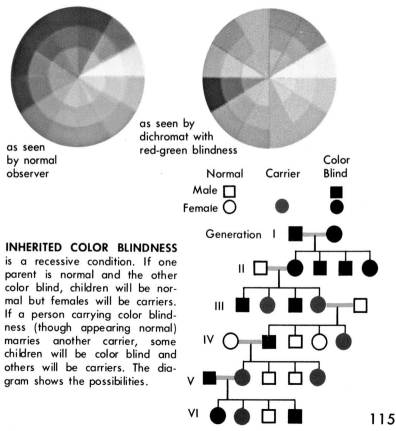

as seen by normal observer

as seen by dichromat with red-green blindness

INHERITED COLOR BLINDNESS is a recessive condition. If one parent is normal and the other color blind, children will be normal but females will be carriers. If a person carrying color blindness (though appearing normal) marries another carrier, some children will be color blind and others will be carriers. The diagram shows the possibilities.

115

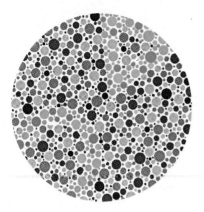
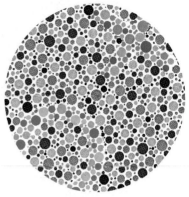

DICHROMATIC COLOR BLIND-ness (p. 115) can be detected by the use of specially colored test plates, each containing a pattern or number made of dots against a background of dots of another color or gray. A person with normal color vision can see the patterns. One with defective color vision will find some of the patterns confusing or absent because of his inability to distinguish the colors of which the patterns are made. At the top of this page, two plates used to distinguish red-green color blindness from normal vision are reproduced in their appropriate colors. A person having red-green color blindness sees only gray dots. The type of plates reproduced at the bottom of the page are used to diagnose blue-yellow defects. These reproductions cannot be employed for valid tests because special inks and printing techniques must be used to achieve the exact hues seen as gray by color-blind individuals. A doctor's charts are more accurate.

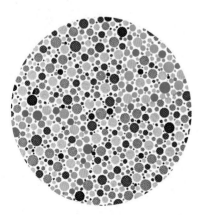
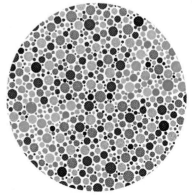

STANDARDS are necessary to be sure that all testing for color vision takes place under standard viewing conditions. The illumination is important. For example, the results might differ depending on whether the tests took place under artificial light or in sunlight.

Two color samples that appear to match under illumination A may not match under illumination B, even though a normal observer says that illumination A matches illumination B. To avoid this difficulty, standard light sources (p. 17) are used for illumination of samples. Under such standard lighting conditions, all observers would still not see the same thing. But by averaging the visual characteristics of many individuals, a composite "standard observer" has been developed who always sees things in the same way. The International Commission on Illumination (see p. 130) has devised a standard observer of this nature. This fictitious individual is simply a set of visual sensitivity curves and energy distribution data by which the results of color experiments can be calculated and standardized.

A luminous efficiency curve shows the ability of different wavelengths to stimulate vision. Thus it is the spectral sensitivity curve for humans. Luminous efficiency curves normally fall between the limits shown here (curves a and b). Humans rarely match exactly the curve (c) of the fictitious standard observer.

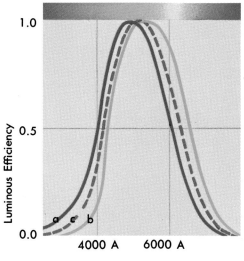

117

COLOR PERCEPTION

Color perception depends largely on human physiology. Man has three visual pigments, each in different cone-shaped receptor cells. One pigment senses primarily blue light, one primarily green, and one primarily red. These cone-shaped cells are tightly packed in the foveal region but are intermixed with rod-shaped cells elsewhere in the retina. Because of these three pigments, man is able to discriminate among a wide range of colors. Their presence was postulated in 1801, but they have only recently been identified within the retina.

Previously it was thought that the impulses from the cones traveled three discrete pathways to the brain. Evidence now indicates that impulses from the three types of receptor cones are somehow combined into a coded signal prior to transmission from the eye to higher visual centers in the brain. The combination takes place in the ganglion cells, nerve cells located on the opposite side of the retina from the cone cells. Changes in wavelength or intensity of the color stimulus change the patterns of coded signals.

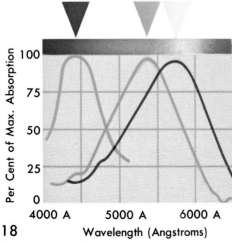

The three cone pigments that sense blue, green, and red have spectral sensibility curves with peaks at 4,470 A (blue-violet), at 5,400 A (green), and at 5,770 A (yellow). Even though the red receptor pigment has its peak in the yellow, it extends into the red so the brain senses red.

MODES OF PERCEPTION

Color is perceived as belonging to a light source when the light source is included in the field of view (1). This is called the illuminant mode of color perception.

In the illumination mode of color perception, the light source is not in the scene, but the direction and quality of the light is evident from the pattern and contrast of the shadows (2).

The object mode of color perception occurs when light is diffusely reflected from an object, and we perceive the color of the surface (3). The color perceived depends partly on nearby objects.

The volume mode of color perception occurs when light passes through a translucent or transparent substance such as a colored liquid or glass (4). Internal qualities predominate rather than the surface ones.

The fundamental or aperture mode of color perception occurs if an object is viewed through an opening that excludes the surroundings (5). Simplest and most easily reproduced, this method is often used in experimental work.

Colors of objects appear different under different illumination even though to the observer the lights appear to be the same. White incandescent light illuminates objects on left. Complementary red and blue-green sources, which appear white to the observer, produced the illumination on the right.

COLOR CONSTANCY is a term used to describe the ability of the human eye to compensate for ordinary changes in illumination and viewing conditions that affect the color of a particular object.

You can tell the color of an object by looking at it under white light. Under a different illumination you may still be able to tell the color of the object, but perhaps not so easily. Light and color reflected from the object may vary greatly with changes in illumination. A yellow book in the sunlight reflects relatively much more blue light than does the same book under an incandescent lamp, but our eyes have little trouble in recognizing the same book and the same object color. This is color constancy. Because of this remarkable property of human vision, you recognize and identify objects in spite of widely different conditions of illumination. Color constancy is evidently a form of eye adaptation to the prevailing illumination. The eye adapts similarly to changes in brightness (p. 32).

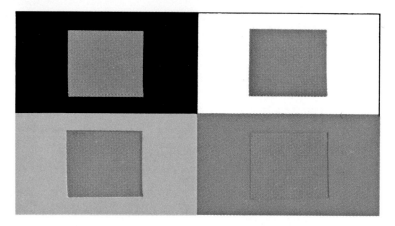

The blue patches in each of the four rectangles are the same size and color. They appear to be different, however, because of simultaneous contrast between them and the colors around them.

CONTRAST increases when two colors are placed side by side. Their difference seems exaggerated. If an orange is presented next to a yellow, for instance, the orange will appear redder and the yellow greener. This is simultaneous color contrast, which accounts for the fine discrimination of the human eye in color matching. Two colors that seem to be identical when viewed separately will often be found quite different if presented side by side.

A similar effect (successive color contrast) occurs if the samples are presented one after the other in quick succession. These two effects (simultaneous and successive contrast) are related. In color matching, your gaze moves rapidly back and forth from one sample to the other when you view them side by side. All your seeing is done with a natural scanning motion, and never with a completely fixed gaze. Both effects enhance the contrast between colors of different hue, causing each to move toward the complementary of the other.

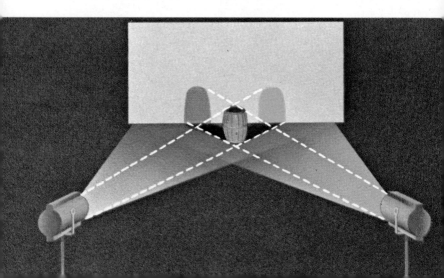

SIMULTANEOUS CONTRAST effects occur not only when two samples are different in hue, but also when the samples are identical in hue but differ in saturation (above). Their difference in saturation is accentuated, and the one of lower saturation on the right tends to acquire the complementary hue.

When two light sources, one white and one of any hue, produce separate shadows of the same object, then each shadow is illuminated by one of the lights—the one not producing the shadow. The background is illuminated by both of them and appears in the hue and saturation of the combined illumination. Under such conditions, the two shadows will tend to appear complementary to each other. The white-illuminated shadow on the left (below) actually appears magenta in contrast with the green-illuminated shadow on the right. This is an interesting example of simultaneous color contrast.

AN AFTERIMAGE is the visual sensation observed after a light stimulus has been removed.

A negative afterimage is a phenomenon that is caused essentially by fatigue in some part of the visual system. As your eyes adapt to a particular color there is a decrease in their sensitivity to that color. When your gaze is shifted to a neutral area, an afterimage appears which is complementary to the original stimulus. This is called a negative afterimage.

Hold this book at reading distance and stare at the cross in the green circle (above). Then look at the dot to the left. You will see a magenta ring. Look at the cross in the red circle (below) and then at the dot to its right to see a green negative afterimage.

A positive afterimage is a far more fleeting experience and difficult to produce. One way is to stand in brilliant sunlight with your eyes closed and further covered by your hand. Remove your hand and gaze quickly (for about 2 or 3 seconds) at either of the circles on this page (warning: do not look at the sun!). Close your eyes immediately and you may get the impression that you are seeing a circle of the same color behind your eyelids. This positive afterimage will seldom last longer than 5 to 10 seconds. It is caused by the persistence of color vision.

123

SUCCESSIVE AFTERIMAGES, neither positive nor negative, are seen if you look steadily at an unshaded light bulb. After a few seconds, put out the light. For a short time afterward, as you sit in the darkness, you will see a succession of varying bright colors. These colors have no apparent relationship to the white light stimulus. If, instead of sitting in darkness, you turn from the light bulb to gaze at a uniform white surface, the colored afterimages you see will become progressively more complementary to those seen in the dark.

SPREADING EFFECT, illustrated below, is a seeming contradiction to simultaneous color contrast (p. 121), in which the contrast between two colors increases when they are placed side by side. The same red ink was used throughout the top strip and the same blue was used throughout the bottom. From what happens during simultaneous contrast, you might expect that the black ink next to the red would make the red appear lighter, or the white next to the red would produce a darker red. Due to the spreading effect, however, the opposite occurs. The blues surrounded by white appear less saturated, too, than those surrounded by black. The spreading effect, as well as the phenomena of afterimages may be the result of the bleaching of cone pigments in the retina, and their subsequent diffusion into neighboring cone cells.

Experts have long sought a foolproof system for specifying color. They would like to identify or describe the color of an object or light so that it can be reproduced with accuracy at another place or time. To do this they must be able to state the color in terms so unequivocal that a color match can be made with reasonable certainty within limits that are visually acceptable. Ideally, the system would work, whether the object being observed was a ball of wool, an automobile with a glossy finish, or a liquid dye. The mode of observation (p. 119) should not affect the color match.

Obviously, no color dictionary can handle the full range of colors. The best in use today includes less than 4,000 color names, although some 10 million colors are said to be distinguishable. A volume of named color samples might be useful within the paint or textile industries. But those samples probably would not duplicate the many glossy and metallic colors used on automobiles today.

Of the three systems described on the following pages, the Munsell, the Ostwald and the CIE, the last is the most complex but the least subjective and provides the high degree of color-matching accuracy many technicians require.

SPECIFYING COLOR is made more difficult because color is influenced by texture. As seen in this illustration, the colors of all the objects match the color sample. Under actual conditions, they might not because surface texture varies from object to object, making their colors appear different.

burgundy

125

THE MUNSELL COLOR SYSTEM was originally devised by Albert H. Munsell, a painter and art teacher. It is an ordered array of colored paper samples. Munsell used three color variables: hue, chroma, and value. Chroma corresponds approximately to saturation (p. 102); value is related to the lightness (p. 35) of the sample. Hues are arranged in spectral order around a circle. The axis of the circle is a ten-step value scale, black at the bottom, through nine shades of gray, to white at the top. Chroma varies along the radii from a minimum at the central achromatic axis to a maximum at the perimeter.

In practice the Munsell System is an atlas of 100 separate pages of paper chips, arranged treelike about the vertical (value) axis. The chips on any one page are all of the same hue, but vary in chroma from left to right and in value from bottom to top. The differences between neighboring samples have been chosen to represent psychologically equal intervals. The Munsell System is an atlas of surface colors. Its reliability depends somewhat upon the surface texture of the color sample being compared. For best results, of course, a standard white source of illumination must be used.

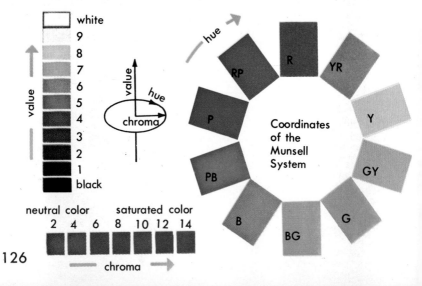

THE MUNSELL COLOR TREE consists of 100 vertical sections, one of which is shown below. Arrow points to color chip identified as 5B 4/8 (hue—5B, value—4, chroma—8).

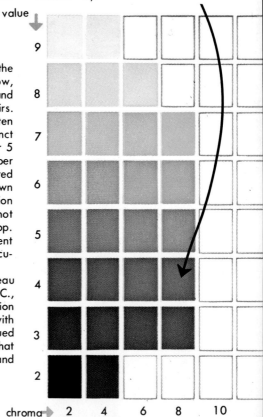

value

vertical section➡

THE TEN BASIC HUES of the Munsell system are red, yellow, green, blue, and purple and combinations of these in pairs. For each hue there are ten gradations, making 100 distinct hues. Each basic hue is number 5 in its gradation scale. Number 10Y is followed by 1GY. Colored samples for basic blue are shown at right. The value designation ranges from 1 at the bottom (not shown) through 9 at the top. Chroma scales are of different lengths, depending on the particular hue and value.

For sale by the National Bureau of Standards, Washington, D.C., and useful in color specification are 18 charts covered with glossy colored chips. Issued with the charts is a table that lists chip number, color name, and Munsell notation.

chroma➡ 2 4 6 8 10

THE OSTWALD COLOR SYSTEM is a material system using color samples similar to those of the Munsell. Like the Munsell system it bears the inherent weakness of printed colors that cannot completely represent those proposed by the system. This weakness is balanced by having a system that is well keyed to the CIE system (pp. 130–132) and in which samples can be directly viewed and matched. The Ostwald system is based on surface colors and is often preferred by artists.

The Ostwald system uses the psychophysical variables of dominant wavelength, purity and luminance instead of the psychological variables of hue, saturation and brightness, as approximated in the Munsell system. Ostwald arranged his system with hues of maximum purity forming an equatorial circle and with complementary colors opposite. The axis of the circle grades from white at the top down to black. In practice, this forms a series of 30 color triangles with a base of lightness and with the most saturated hue at the apex. Each six-sided sample is identified by three numbers representing the proportion of black, white and "full color," adding up to a total of 100 per cent.

Similar in terminology to the Ostwald system is a volume prepared by a bird expert, Robert Ridgway, and used by biologists for over 50 years. The Ridgway color dictionary shows over 1,100 colors with names that indicate full color, tint and shade.

COMPARISON OF OSTWALD AND MUNSELL SYSTEMS

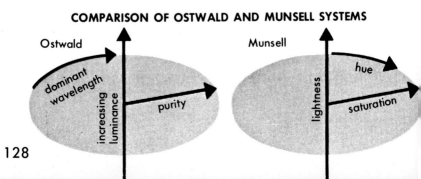

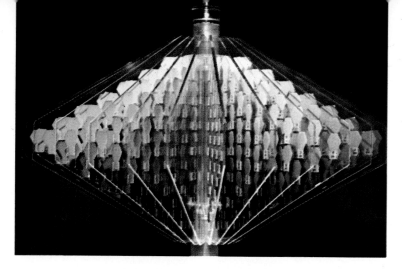

THE OSTWALD COLOR TREE

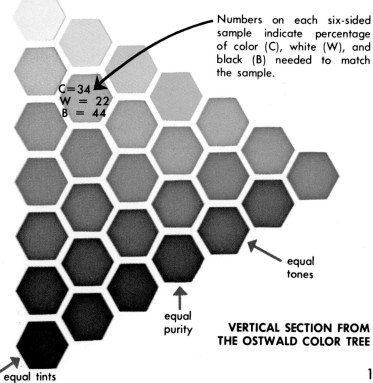

Numbers on each six-sided sample indicate percentage of color (C), white (W), and black (B) needed to match the sample.

C = 34
W = 22
B = 44

equal tones

equal purity

equal tints

VERTICAL SECTION FROM THE OSTWALD COLOR TREE

129

THE CIE SYSTEM makes it possible to describe color samples in mathematical terms and to represent the dominant wavelength and purity of the sample on a diagram. The system was developed by the Commission Internationale de l'Eclairage—CIE (International Commission of Illumination). It deals with dominant wavelength and purity like the Ostwald system (p. 128) and can also be related to the Munsell system (p. 126). Both systems have now been keyed in CIE terms, so notations can usually be converted from one system to the other.

To develop the CIE system, data was needed on the color-matching characteristics of the average eye. Using a colorimeter, a number of observers made a series of color matches against a spectrum of monochromatic colors employing a mixture of three primary colors (specific wavelengths of red, green, and blue). Based on the results, three color mixture curves (below) were produced. These represent the relative amount of each of the primaries needed by the standard observer to match any part of the visible spectrum. By a mathematical transformation, a related set of curves was produced in which the green curve (curve $\bar{y}$) also expresses the luminance observed at each wavelength and is thus also the standard luminosity curve.

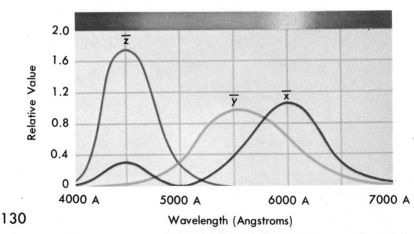

A CHROMATICITY DIAGRAM, developed by the CIE, with values from the three color-mixture curves serves as a pictorial map on which any color can be shown. In practice, the color of any sample is defined by citing its coordinates on the chromaticity diagram (below) and adding a figure for its relative luminance.

To produce the chromaticity diagram, readings were taken from the color-mixture curves at a sufficient number of selected intervals. From these were derived the coordinates for a series of points representing a spectrum of fully saturated colors. Plotting these points and joining them with a smooth curve provided the basic triangular structure of the chromaticity diagram (fig. 1, below).

All visible colors can be represented by points within this figure. The entire spectrum of fully saturated hues lies on the smooth outer curve, ranging from violet (4,000 A) at the lowest point through hues of green (5,200 A) at top to red (7,000 A) at right. Non-spectral purples are found along the line that con-

nects the lower extremities of the curve. Any straight line through the center point C will intersect the curve at complementary wavelengths.

Three standard light sources (p. 17) have been defined and their coordinates also plotted as three points on the chromaticity diagram (fig. 1). These points represent the color characteristics of an ordinary incandescent lamp (A), approximate noon sunlight (B), and average daylight (C). A's position, closer to long (red) wavelengths than C's, shows that indoor lamps appear reddish compared to daylight.

A typical CIE notation for an impure red color sample (fig. 2) might be given as x = 0.58, y = 0.33, and relative luminance (Y) = 0.24.

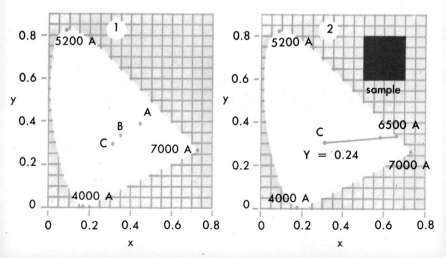

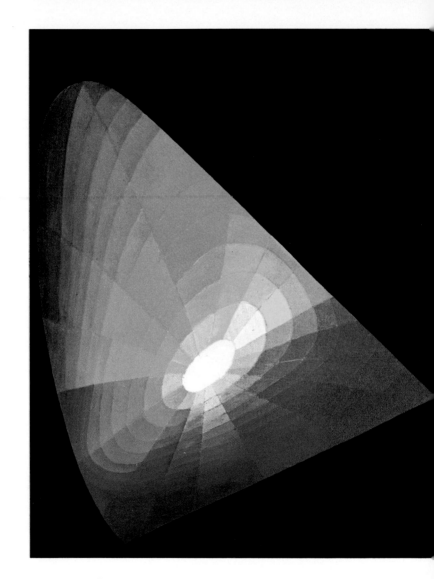

Oil painting by L. Condax, from *The Science of Color*,
copyright 1963 by the Optical Society of America

THE CIE CHROMATICITY DIAGRAM (left) shows colors determined by the CIE graphs and equations. The CIE system works on formulas, not on color samples, but the illustration does give a rough visual indication.

Along the smooth curved perimeter are the colors of the spectrum with much space for greens because the eye is more sensitive to them. Purples lie on the straight line connecting the red and blue ends of the curve. All other colors are represented by points enclosed by the curve.

The achromatic point (white) is near the center. Colors increase in saturation with their distance from the achromatic point. Thus, oval zones around this point represent colors of equal saturation. Each pie-like sector contains a small range of hues, graded by saturation. Hues at opposite ends of any straight line through the center are complementary. An additive mixture of any two colors is represented by an intermediate point somewhere on the straight line between the points representing the two colors.

LIGHT AND COLOR AS TOOLS

Light and color are so much a part of our lives that we often overlook their fundamental importance to many businesses such as advertising, television, photography, paint, printing, optics, and many others. Artists, decorators, and designers use light and color in their creations. The artist's task, for example, is not one of reproduction, but of representation. By lines, and form, and color he seeks to represent those features of a person, a scene, an idea, or an emotion that he feels are interesting or important. He must know and use the symbolism and emotional effect of his colors no matter what his style or school. He must keep in mind the effects of color constancy and color contrast, and he must either apply or purposefully ignore the rules of harmonious color combinations.

Even the realist does not try to paint a scene exactly as he sees it. The picture is not the actual scene, and the viewer's response to the picture may differ from his attitude toward the scene itself.

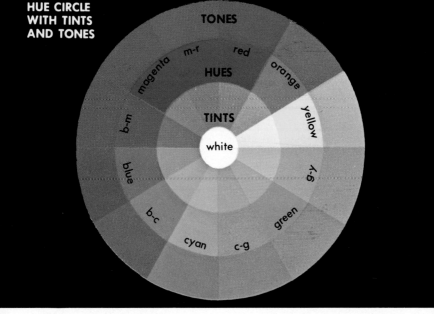

TONES

m-r   red

magenta

orange

HUES

b-m

yellow

TINTS

white

blue

y-g

b-c

green

cyan   c-g

HARMONY AND DISCORD are descriptive terms ordinarily associated with music, but they also apply to color. Harmony and discord in both cases indicate combinations that are pleasant or unpleasant within our culture. Rules of color harmony and discord are derived from experience and sanctioned by social acceptance. They have no known mathematical or scientific basis.

An artist or a decorator may discuss harmony and discord in terms of color circles of tints, hues, and tones. Tints are produced when white is added to saturated hues. Adding black, instead, produces tones or shades. Adjacent colors and opposing complementary hues on the circles harmonize fairly well. Widely separated hues, not complementary, tend to produce discord.

All fully saturated colors do not appear to have the same degree of saturation. A saturated yellow appears

HARMONIOUS HUES include yellow and green (1), close on the hue circle, and complementary blue and yellow (2).

DISCORDANT HUES, such as magenta and yellow (3), are far apart on the hue circle, but not far enough to be complementary.

much brighter than does its complementary saturated blue. Simultaneously, the range of colors from a pale yellow tint to a fully saturated yellow seems greater than from a pale blue tint to a darker, fully saturated blue. Normally a saturated blue seems pleasant near a less saturated yellow. The reverse situation, placing a fully saturated yellow next to a less saturated blue, appears unpleasant even though the two colors are complementary. While adjacent colors of the hue circle blend fairly well, they tend to make a bland and uninteresting composition. Artists will often add a splash of color from a different part of the spectrum, a deliberate discord, to give spice and emphasis to a scene.

DISCORDANT APPEARANCE of two usually harmonious colors is due to the difference in saturation. The yellow is fully saturated and the blue is not (4).

Equal areas of red and cyan (5) are discordant as shown. The same colors are used in (6), but the cyan is dominant and the combination is harmonious.

Custom decrees that boy babies be dressed in blue, girl babies in pink; that brides wear white and mourning widows wear black.

THE SYMBOLISM OF COLOR has developed over the years as certain colors have become associated with special meanings. In general, dark, saturated colors give a feeling of richness and elegance. Bright, saturated colors express liveliness and gaiety. Dark, unsaturated colors are sad and moody, while light unsaturated ones tend toward frivolity and cheerfulness.

Literature and custom tell us that reddish hues are warm; bluish ones are cold. Red is the color of anger and courage. White stands for purity, innocence, and hope. Green is the color of youth and vigor, but also of envy and inexperience. Yellow suggests cowardice, also cheerfulness and sunshine. Blue can be puritanical, moody, indecent, or true. Passion is frequently purple, but violet purple has the dignity of royalty, while reddish purple is the color of rage.

Colors often have different meanings in different cultures. In Western cultures, black expresses wickedness, sorrow, and despair. It is a funeral color, while in China mourners wear white. The Aztecs associated colors with the four compass points, North being red. Emotional associations with color may be an individual and not a cultural matter, and two people may often find their tastes in conflict.

PAINTS, used to protect or to decorate surfaces, consist of finely ground pigment particles suspended in a liquid, the vehicle. The pigment particles (p. 138) are white or colored, and are usually opaque.

The vehicle helps to spread the paint evenly, and, when dry, binds or glues the pigment to the surface. The oil paint used by artists is a pigment paste in a vehicle of linseed or poppyseed oil that is thinned with turpentine. A familiar vehicle of household paints is linseed oil. The paint is thinned, most commonly with turpentine or a petroleum derivative. The thinner may also speed up drying. In newer paints the vehicle is a rubber-based, fast-drying compound, or some plastic such as a vinyl or acrylic type. The type of vehicle used may affect the degree of gloss or the flatness of the paint, and thus the appearance or color of the surface painted. A glossy or enamel paint on a smooth-textured surface is shiny due to regular reflection of light. The color of a glossy surface is seen most easily when viewed from the direction of the incident light. When viewed from the opposite direction, the gloss tends to hide the color. A flat paint diffuses rather than reflects the light regularly from a surface.

To impart an air of cheerfulness or efficiency to interior walls, paints with high reflectance values (percentage of incident light reflected) are often used. Reflectances of 50–60% are held desirable for schools and offices; 35–55% for the home. Paints that give lower reflectance values (30–40%) can be used for trim, floors, and furniture. The approximate reflectance values for four flat green paints are shown below.

61%   48%   38%   20%

PIGMENTS provide the color and the covering or hiding power of paint. They also contribute to its durability and to the permanency of the color in weathering. Natural, or mineral, pigments are made of finely ground earth materials, such as cinnabar, ochre, charcoal, and others. Pigments may be either organic or inorganic, but most of them are now produced synthetically. The oldest white pigment is white lead, a carbonate of lead made by corroding lead sheets and then collecting and drying the fine powder. Because it has about nine times greater hiding power, and is inert chemically, titanium dioxide is replacing white lead. Some red and many yellow and brown pigments are derived from an iron oxide. The common yellow used by artists, however, is cadmium yellow. A green pigment is produced from chromium oxide; bright Prussian blue is a complex iron cyanide. Black is made of finely divided lampblack (carbon).

Paint extenders are white or nearly white pigments that add little or no color to the paint, but help to give it body. Metals in powder form may be added in the vehicle to make various metallic paints. Luminous paints contain pigments or dyes that glow when illuminated, as by automobile headlights.

When a beam of white light strikes a painted surface, some light is reflected, part of it penetrates and is absorbed. The remainder is diffusely reflected and is responsible for the color you see.

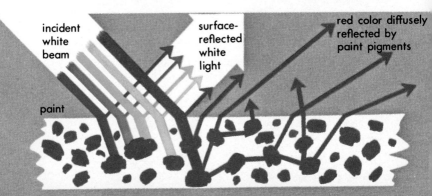

incident white beam

surface-reflected white light

red color diffusely reflected by paint pigments

paint

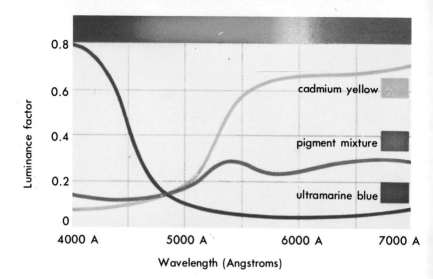

Spectral reflection curve for a mixture of two parts of cadmium yellow (upper curve) with one part of ultramarine blue (lower curve) does not show pure effects of either additive or subtractive mixing. Middle curve is the blended paint.

Pigments do not dissolve, nor do they unite chemically with the paint vehicle. If two pigments are mixed in a paint, the color of the paint appears to change though it still consists of the two distinct pigments. This effect is due to additive color mixing (p. 107). The mixing of paints to obtain desired colors is complicated because not only additive but also subtractive color mixing (p. 110) is involved. A successful prediction of the results usually requires much experience. In fact, one of the problems of the paint industry is to determine how to relate the color of a paint mixture to the spectral reflection characteristics of its component pigments. Results cannot be predicted on the basis of the curves from the component pigments. A partial understanding comes from knowledge about the relative amounts of scattering and absorption that occur in the pigments.

DYES are colorants. Unlike pigments, they are soluble, and the particles of the dye are of molecular size and cannot be seen even with the most powerful optical microscope.

Most dyes can be applied directly, particularly to the animal fibers, such as wool and silk. Others are effective only if the fiber is treated first with a dye fastener, or mordant, a chemical that causes the dye colors to adhere to the fibers. Cotton and linen usually require a mordant. Synthetic fibers often involve complex dyeing problems.

Nearly all dyes are organic compounds. Originally they were made from fruits, flowers, bark, roots, insects, and marine mollusks. A few used in earlier days were of mineral origin, but most used today are produced synthetically. The first of these was an aniline dye, discovered accidentally in 1866. This beautiful mauve dye was the beginning of the enormous coal-tar dye industry that today produces nearly all dyestuffs.

About 4,000 different dyes are available commercially. These fit into 22 chemical classes and are each identified by dye experts with a five-digit number. Dyes are classified chemically, but also by their color, by the materials they color, and by the dyeing methods used. The ultraviolet rays of sunlight break down many dyes into colorless compounds. A good dye resists fading. Dyes must also resist the reaction of detergents and other household chemicals. Dyes that are not easily removed are known as fast dyes. To get suitable dyes for a great number of fabrics and other materials with a variety of textures, computers are now used to summarize the variables.

The problems of dyeing are largely practical. The difference between the absorption curve of the dye and the reflection curve of the dyed material attest to the fact that the color of the dye solution and of the dyed material are often quite different. In viewing and matching dyed materials, standard illumination is important, as every woman knows who takes a skirt to the window where she can see its true daylight color.

CHROMOPHORES, groups of atoms that contain loosely held electrons capable of selectively absorbing some wavelengths from white light and transmitting the rest, give color to organic dyes. Since only a portion of the wavelengths contained in white light remains and reaches your eyes, the light from the dye appears colored. Chromophores are found in all colored organic compounds, or chromogens. To convert a chromogen to a dye, another group of atoms, the auxochrome, must be present. These atoms fix (attach) the dye to a fabric. Elements of the structural formula of the dye called Butter Yellow are shown below.

A chromophore in a chromogen + an auxochrome = a dye

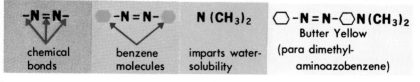

$-N=N-$	$-N=N-$	$N(CH_3)_2$	⬡$-N=N-$⬡$N(CH_3)_2$
			Butter Yellow
chemical bonds	benzene molecules	imparts water-solubility	(para dimethyl-aminoazobenzene)

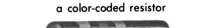

| 0 | 1 | 2 | 3 | 4 | 5 | 6 | 7 | 8 | 9 |

COLOR IN BUSINESS AND INDUSTRY has many uses. Showing debit figures in red ink and credits in black ink is an example of color coding. A more elaborate code is used to mark electronic resistors and capacitors. Each numeral is assigned a unique color (above), so that a sequence of bands or dots can be used to indicate the value of a component. A 25,000-ohm resistor is marked as shown below. Red stands for the two, green for the five, and orange, in this position, means the number ends in three zeros. The silver band indicates that the resistor value is accurate within 10 per cent.

a color-coded resistor

COLOR CODES may be used to distinguish the different circuits in electrical wiring. Some codes are for convenience and efficiency, while others are primarily for safety. One of the most common color codes in existence is the red, yellow, and green traffic light.

The use of accurate color matching devices allows chemists to analyze samples rapidly or to control quality. Color is the key to the temperature of furnaces and to the testing or grading of food products such as tomatoes or bananas.

Mass production often demands that parts manufactured at different places match in color when finally assembled. This requires elaborate methods of color control.

Color coding is evident in the electronic circuit at left and in the wires that make up the telephone cable below.

In packaging, what's outside counts most. The design and color on the exterior often determine the success or failure of a product. Bold hues aid in the "hard sell."

COLOR IN ADVERTISING has three uses: to attract attention, to decorate, and to influence by symbolism. Bright colors and contrast are more important in catching the eye of a prospective customer than a brand name or slogan. The brand name is read after the eye has been caught, and often after the customer has picked up the package in his hand. An attractive appearance can often sell an inferior product. Manufacturers spend millions of dollars each year to ensure that their products are decorated to the customer's taste, knowing that many times a simple change in color has meant the difference between commercial success and failure.

The powerful symbolism of different colors can strongly affect the decision to buy or reject. A yellow soap, for instance, may be thought stronger than a white soap, perhaps because yellow is symbolic of power. A man may buy cigarettes in a red package, but avoid them if the package is pink—because the color is not a "masculine" one. In recent years, a major gasoline company decided that it needed a more aggressive marketing approach and changed its trade colors from a tame green and white to a bold red, white, and blue at a cost of millions of dollars. Color may even be the deciding factor in the choice of an expensive car.

143

PHOTOGRAPHY depends on a photochemical reaction in an emulsion of silver halide crystals embedded in gelatin. Light rays produce a latent image in the emulsion which is reduced to pure silver by treatment with a developer. After development, the unreduced silver halide is removed by the fixing process. The resulting image consists of a deposit of pure silver embedded in hardened gelatin. The density of the deposit is determined by the exposure. This is a negative image because it is dark where the original scene was light, and light where the original scene was dark. To produce a positive image, light is passed through this negative onto another photographic emulsion, either on film or on paper.

If the original developed film is not fixed, but is bleached instead, a uniform exposure of the film to light will then produce a positive latent image which may be developed in the usual way. This reversal process is used for many amateur color films, both movie and still. Black and white photographic emulsions are often more sensitive to one color than to another. By dye-sensitizing, they can be made more sensitive to different wavelengths, as desired.

COLOR NEGATIVE shows maximum density and deepest color where image is lightest. In a subtractive film the colors on the negative are complementary to the color of the image.

COLOR POSITIVE is made by placing a sheet of color film or paper behind the negative and exposing them to light. When the film or paper is developed, a positive color image results.

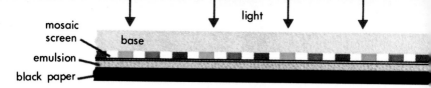

Cross-section of additive, three-color, mosaic system camera film

COLOR PHOTOGRAPHY done for commercial purposes uses dyes or colored filters, and nearly all involve three separate images made by exposure to light from three different parts of the spectrum. Color processes differ mainly in methods of making and combining the images.

The three main methods in use today are the color negative (p. 144), direct reversal (which produces transparencies, p. 146), and color separation. The last involves making a separate negative for each color, and its use is restricted exclusively to the printing and commercial picture industries (p. 149).

ADDITIVE COLOR emulsions (Dufaycolor) often use a fine-grained mosaic of microscopic red, blue, and green dots. Light from the image passes through these dots to reach the emulsion, a light-sensitive layer of silver halide. The silver halide crystals are affected by the pattern of the image coming through the colored dots.

When the film is developed, the darker areas turn to metal-lic silver and are removed, leaving a positive transparency. The transparent dots, too small to be seen individually on projection, fuse visually into hues approximating those of the image.

The Dufaycolor film used to make the accompanying photograph was covered with a cross-hatching of fine lines, as many as 1,000 to the inch, each dyed red, green, or blue. It is an obsolete, additive color process.

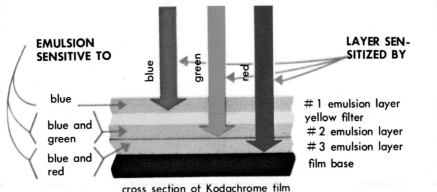

EMULSION
SENSITIVE TO

blue   green   red

LAYER SEN-
SITIZED BY

blue ⟶ #1 emulsion layer
         yellow filter
blue and green ⟶ #2 emulsion layer
blue and red ⟶ #3 emulsion layer
         film base

cross section of Kodachrome film

COMMON COLOR FILMS, such as Kodachrome, Ektachrome, and Anscochrome, contain three different emulsion layers and a yellow filter. In Kodachrome (above) the first layer of emulsion is sensitive to blue light, the second to blue and green, and the third to blue and red. But the yellow filter, between the first and second emulsion layers, blocks the blue light, allowing only red and green to pass through. As a result, the second emulsion layer is sensitized only by green light, and the third layer only by red. In this way, three negative images representing the three primary colors are formed simultaneously.

During development, the silver in each image is replaced by the appropriate dye, and the yellow filter is bleached out. Because the images are negative, each layer must be dyed its complementary color to form positive images. The blue sensitive emulsion layer is dyed yellow, the blue and green sensitive layer is dyed magenta, and the blue and red sensitive layer is dyed cyan.

Kodachrome photograph

In Kodachrome, the dye-forming chemicals (called couplers) are contained in the developer, and processing is quite complicated. The final color transparency is normally pleasing, and resolution of detail is exceptionally good. In other multilayer films, the dye couplers are contained in the emulsions. The three-color images can be developed all at once in the same developer, a process well within the capability of many amateurs.

POLACOLOR FILM, introduced in 1963, enables one to obtain a finished color print one minute after taking the picture. The multilayer Polacolor negative is exposed in a Polaroid Land Camera. Processing occurs inside of the camera for the roll films and outside of the camera in a light-tight sandwich for the pack film.

A POLACOLOR FILM assembly (1) consists of the negative, the pod and the receiving sheet (positive). The negative contains three emulsion layers, each sensitive to a different region of the spectrum. Next to each layer is a layer containing yellow, magenta, or cyan dye-developer molecules. In the pod is a thick, jelly-like processing reagent to activate the dye-developers. The finished color positive is formed on the receiving sheet.

After exposure, the film assembly is pulled through a set of rollers (2) that burst the pod and spread the reagent between the negative and the receiving sheet (3). Wherever light has activated an emulsion layer, dye-developer molecules become trapped in the negative. Wherever the emulsion has not been affected by light, the dye-developer molecules continue through the negative to the receiving sheet where they are locked in place to form a positive color print (below).

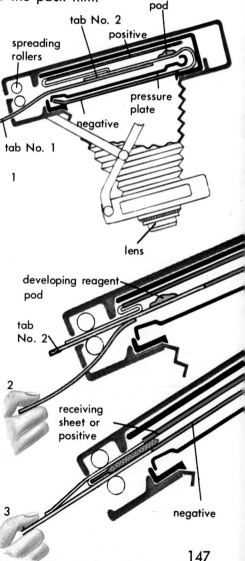

pod

tab No. 2

positive

spreading rollers

pressure plate

negative

tab No. 1

1

lens

developing reagent pod

tab No. 2

2

receiving sheet or positive

3

negative

PRINTING is one of the most important methods of communication using light and color. This ancient art probably began with hand-carved wooden blocks pressed against an inky surface and then applied to paper. The use of movable type put printing on a mass production basis. Now, photo-typesetting, often controlled by a computer, is replacing type. High-speed presses turn out newspapers, magazines and books at speeds greater than 1,500 feet per minute. About a billion books and about 2.5 billion magazines are printed annually in the U.S.

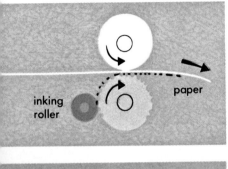

LETTERPRESS, derived from the original method of printing from carved blocks, prints from a raised surface. Type is made with elevated letters; photographs are translated into patterns of raised dots. Many newspapers are printed by letterpress, with a typesetting device—the Linotype machine—using raised letters.

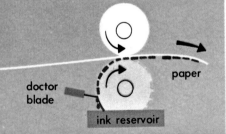

GRAVURE is the reverse of letterpress. Ink is picked up from depressions in the plate. Gravure developed from intaglio where the letters or designs were carved into wood. The plate is inked, then wiped so that ink remains only in the pits until it is picked up by the paper in printing. Printing off of rotary plates—rotogravure—is very rapid.

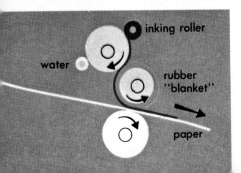

LITHOGRAPHY, originally printing from a stone, now imprints both illustration and text from relatively smooth metal plates.

To reproduce a photograph or other picture with light and shade, the illustration is photographed through a camera that has a

Full-color printing of Gauguin's self portrait requires three color plates and one black. Dots are aligned at a different angle to be sure they do not print on one another.

rotatable screen. The criss-crossing ruled lines of the screen produce a series of dots on the negative. The finer the screen, the better the detail. Newspapers use a 65-line screen (65 dots per linear inch). This book uses 133.

To make your eyes register the dots as a continuous tone value, the camera screen is set so that the parallel rows of dots on the negative occur at some angle to the horizontal. For black or any single color halftone, the angle is 45 degrees.

In full-color reproduction, the illustration is photographed through blue, green, and red filters, producing a separate negative for each color. The dots are large where the original color is saturated; small where it is weak. A printing plate is made for each negative, the process being very similar to printing a photograph from a negative, but a metal plate coated with a light-sensitive emulsion is used instead of photographic paper.

Neither a raised nor a depressed surface is needed on the metal plates used in lithographic printing. Instead, each plate is waxy or otherwise repels the ink except at those places where letters or designs appear.

Yellow, magenta, and cyan inks, complementary in color to the filters, are used with the plates to duplicate the original illustration. Sometimes the overlap of these three inks does not give a strong black, so a black-and-white halftone is usually added. Four-color separations were used for many of the illustrations in this book as shown above.

IN OFFSET LITHOGRAPHY, the roller-mounted plate becomes inked as it revolves. Its image is transferred (offset) in reverse onto a rubber mat or "blanket" which encircles another cylinder. As this mat turns, it transfers the now unreversed image onto paper held firm during the moment of impression by a counter-rotating third cylinder, A separate three-cylinder unit operates for each color.

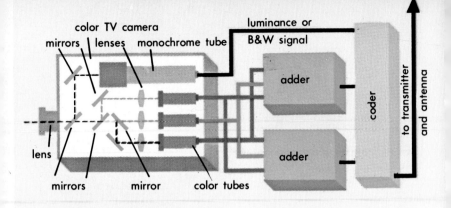

The color TV camera records the scene in three primary colors.

COLOR TELEVISION employs a mosaic method of additive color mixing (p. 109). The image is produced by the action of a beam of swift electrons on a fluorescent screen. The fine beam of electrons sweeps across the screen 525 times for each picture, and 30 pictures are presented each second. To achieve satisfactory definition, the intensity of the electron beam is modulated at frequencies up to 4.5 million cycles per second (4½ megacycles). The large bandwidth of this frequency means that the transmitting station must use carrier waves less than 10 feet long. (AM radio waves are about 1,000 feet long.)

In the television studio, the color camera views a scene through a system of color separating (dichroic) mirrors, producing a separate electronic signal for each primary color. About 20 per cent of the light that enters the camera bypasses its three color tubes and is directed to a monochrome tube. The signal from this latter tube contains most of the information needed to produce picture detail and brightness. After the signals leave the camera, they combine to modulate the carrier wave, which is then broadcast by a transmitter and antenna.

ELECTROMAGNETIC WAVES transmitted from the television station are picked up by the antenna of the receiver, and are separated into the three original color components and the monochrome (black and white) portion by electronic circuits. The color components are converted into three small voltages used to control the emission of electrons from three electron guns, one for each color component. The electrons themselves do not carry color characteristics, but represent the voltages produced by the light entering the camera. The color screen of the receiver is covered by rows of three-dot clusters of phosphors that emit red, blue, or green light when excited by an electron (p. 24). The amount of light emitted is related to the number of electrons that strike the phosphor.

The dots in each cluster are arranged so the electrons from the green gun always strike the phosphor that emits green light, those from the red gun always strike the phosphor that emits red light and those from the blue gun excite the phosphor that emits blue light. As different voltages are supplied to the red, blue and green guns, varying levels of each color are emitted by the phosphor clusters. Since the dots are very small and close together, they cannot be resolved separately by the eye, but are mixed by mosaic fusion (p. 109) into the hue that was originally seen in that area of the picture by the camera. As all of the rows of three-dot clusters are scanned, a colored picture is produced.

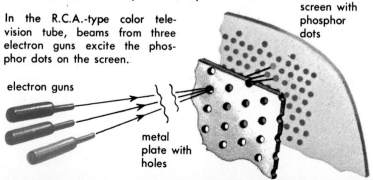

In the R.C.A.-type color television tube, beams from three electron guns excite the phosphor dots on the screen.

screen with phosphor dots

electron guns

metal plate with holes

Beam from ruby laser

LASERS produce an intense, monochromatic beam of light that can be focused to weld, melt, or vaporize a small amount of any substance. They may be used in communications, in the acceleration of chemical reactions, and in surgery. Laser is an acronym for "light amplification by stimulated emission of radiation." The first laser was built in 1960.

Lasers emit coherent (in-step) light waves, whereas an ordinary light source radiates light of mixed wavelengths in an out-of-step (noncoherent) and random manner. The luminance of the image of ordinary light cannot exceed the source's luminance. But a laser can form a very luminant image because its parallel rays can be focused to a tiny spot and are added together in phase.

Pencil-thin laser beam is used in optical and mechanical alignment.

The light from a small laser, in fact, can be focused to form an image of luminance greater than that of the sun's surface. The concentration of energy is so great that extremely high temperatures are produced. Light rays from a laser can be beamed through space with a fraction of an inch spread per mile. The light is also extremely pure in color (monochromatic).

IN A RUBY LASER (below) a ruby crystal rod has plane parallel polished ends which are silvered like mirrors. One end is only partially silvered and acts as a window for the light to get out. Energy is supplied to the ruby crystal by a powerful flash tube lamp. This serves to pump the (chromium) atoms of the crystal to a "metastable" energy state in which they linger for a few thousandths of a second before dropping to the ground state with the emission of a photon of light. Most of these photons pass out of the crystal walls and are lost, but soon one photon will move directly along the rod and is reflected from the polished ends, passing back and forth along the rod until it encounters an atom in the excited metastable state. The excited atom then radiates its photon in exact phase with the photon which struck it. This second photon may in turn stimulate another atom, and this "cascade" process continues until the whole crystal is filled with in-phase radiation oscillating back and forth inside the rod. Part of this radiation is emitted through the half-silvered end of the rod and becomes the laser beam. All of this takes place within a few billionths of a second, then the flash tube fires again and the process is repeated.

Modern lasers have been made of solid crystals, glass, liquids and gases. Some operate in pulses as described, but many emit continuously. In all, the radiation is monochromatic and coherent. It is this high degree of coherence that makes laser light different from that of all other sources.

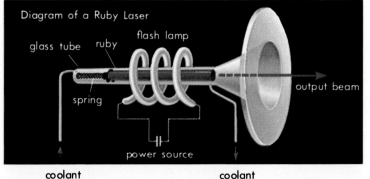

Diagram of a Ruby Laser

glass tube   ruby   flash lamp

spring

output beam

power source

coolant   coolant

HOLOGRAPHY is a special kind of photography in which the film captures not the image of the subject but the pattern of the wavefronts of light reflected from the subject. Invented by Dennis Gabor in 1948, the process took on new importance when the laser was invented. In addition to its uses in the entertainment field, holography has many scientific and industrial applications, which are being developed rapidly.

TO MAKE A HOLOGRAM, a coherent light beam (from a laser) is split into two parts—an object beam which illuminates the subject, and a reference beam which is directed to the photographic film by mirrors. At the film the light reflected from the subject interferes with the reference beam to cause a complex pattern of light and dark fringes in the film when it is developed.

When a hologram is held in a beam of coherent light, part of the diffracted light is a reproduction of the original light wave pattern that came from the subject. Thus, a viewer looking through the hologram can see a life-like reproduction of the original scene. This virtual image is truly three-dimensional, since the viewer can move his head and see a different perspective of the subject. Besides the virtual image, there is also a real image formed by the rays diffracted in another direction.

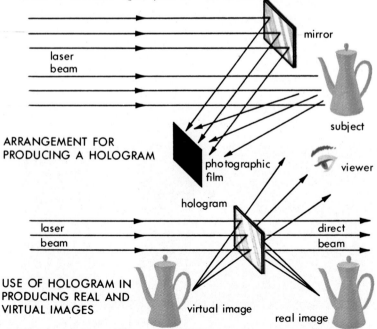

laser beam

mirror

subject

ARRANGEMENT FOR PRODUCING A HOLOGRAM

photographic film

viewer

hologram

laser beam

direct beam

USE OF HOLOGRAM IN PRODUCING REAL AND VIRTUAL IMAGES

virtual image

real image

FIBER OPTICS is the result of an ingenious application of a simple principle. Imagine a light ray that has entered the end of a slim solid glass rod. If it always strikes the surface of the glass at angles greater than the critical angle (p. 44), the ray will be totally reflected each time and trapped within the glass. Reflected from side to side, the light ray will be conducted along the rod like water in a hose. Finally, the light ray hits the end of the rod at a small angle to the perpendicular and

light ray traveling through fiber

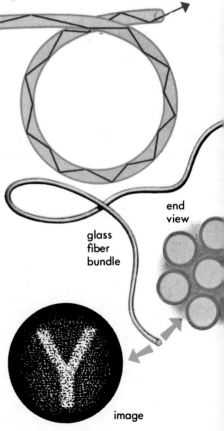

glass fiber bundle

end view

image

A big advance in fiber optics came with the development of very fine clear fibers encased in a thin coating of lower refractive index. Total reflection takes place between the fiber and its coating. The fibers are so thin (a few microns in diameter) that they are flexible, and their coatings allow them to be bound into bundles without interfering with each other's action. Such a bundle can conduct light for several feet. When the fibers are lined up so they have the same relative position at each end of the bundle, they can transmit images. This makes possible a sort of super-periscope so flexible that physicians can use it to examine the interior of body organs. A sheath of unaligned fibers around the bundle can carry illumination to the area being examined.

155

is able to exit. This explains the success of bent lucite and glass rods as light-conductors in advertising displays and in simple illuminating devices.

A bundle of fibers produces a grainy image like a halftone printing process. By drawing out the fibers so that one end of the bundle is smaller than the other, the image can be enlarged or reduced and its brightness changed. The quality of the image can be improved by shaping the end of the bundle or by adjusting the alignment of the fibers to eliminate distortions.

MORE INFORMATION

Burnham, Hanes, Bartleson, COLOR: A GUIDE TO BASIC FACTS AND CONCEPTS, New York, N.Y.: John Wiley & Sons, 1963. A compact handbook of definitions and facts about color.

Committee on Colorimetry, Optical Society of America, THE SCIENCE OF COLOR, New York, N.Y.: Thomas Y. Crowell Co., 1953. A complete authoritative report for the serious student, with extensive reference and glossary.

Eastman Kodak, COLOR AS SEEN AND PHOTOGRAPHED, Rochester, N.Y.: A Kodak Color Data Book, 1966. A brief explanation of color principles and color films.

Evans, Ralph M., AN INTRODUCTION TO COLOR, New York, N.Y.: John Wiley & Sons, 1948. A careful explanation of all aspects of color in non-technical language.

Evans, Ralph M., EYE, FILM, AND CAMERA IN COLOR PHOTOGRAPHY, New York, N.Y.: John Wiley & Sons, 1959. A thorough discussion of visual perception and its relation to photographic representation.

Fowles, Grant R., INTRODUCTION TO MODERN OPTICS, New York, N.Y.: Holt, Rinehart & Winston, 1968. A college textbook that emphasizes the latest developments in optics, including lasers.

Mann, Ida, and A. Pirie, THE SCIENCE OF SEEING, Baltimore, Md.: Pelican Books, 1950. All about eyes and how they work.

Minnaert, M., THE NATURE OF LIGHT AND COLOUR IN THE OPEN AIR, New York, N.Y.: Dover Publications, Inc., 1954. Explanations of shadows, mirages, rainbows and similar phenomena.

Neblette, C. B., PHOTOGRAPHY, ITS MATERIALS AND PROCESSES, 6th Edition, Van Nostrand-Reinhold Books, New York, N.Y.: 1962. An authoritative discussion of all phases of photographic technology.

Sears, Francis W., OPTICS, 3rd Edition, Reading, Mass.: Addison-Wesley, 1949. A popular college textbook with excellent illustrations.

INDEX

Boldface numerals indicate main coverage.

159